PENGUIN BOOKS

FINISH STRONG

Nate Ebner is a two-sport athlete who is the only person to ever compete in the Olympics as an active NFL player and then go on to win a Super Bowl. He has won three Super Bowls with the New England Patriots and participated in the 2016 Summer Olympics in Rio as one of twelve members of the United States rugby team, and he now plays for the New York Giants. In his youth, Ebner bonded with his father through rugby. After Ebner tragically lost his father, he kept his promise to him to walk on to the football team at Ohio State and make it in the NFL.

Paul Daugherty has been the sports columnist at the *Cincinnati Enquirer* since 1994. In 2015, the Associated Press Sports Editors named Daugherty the best columnist and best feature writer in America.

Finish Strong

A FATHER'S CODE
AND A SON'S PATH

Nate Ebner

and Paul Daugherty

Foreword by Urban Meyer

PENGUIN BOOKS

PENGUIN BOOKS
An imprint of Penguin Random House LLC
penguinrandomhouse.com

First published in the United States of America by Penguin Press,
an imprint of Penguin Random House LLC, 2021
Published in Penguin Books 2022

Insert, page 7, bottom, Diamond Images via Getty Images; page 8, © USA TODAY Sports;
page 9, top, Darren McCollester/Getty Images Sport via Getty Images, bottom,
AP Photo/Elise Amendola; page 13, bottom, Sarah A Sall, Photography;
page 14, bottom, Boston Globe via Getty Images; page 15, David Rogers/Getty
Images Sport via Getty Images. All other images courtesy of the author.

ISBN 9780525560876 (paperback)

THE LIBRARY OF CONGRESS HAS CATALOGED THE HARDCOVER EDITION AS FOLLOWS:
Names: Ebner, Nate, 1988– author. | Daugherty, Paul, 1957– author.
Title: Finish strong : a father's code and a son's path / Nate Ebner, Paul Daugherty.
Description: New York : Penguin Press, 2021. |
Identifiers: LCCN 2020028103 (print) | LCCN 2020028104 (ebook) |
ISBN 9780525560852 (hardcover) | ISBN 9780525560869 (ebook)
Subjects: LCSH: Ebner, Nate, 1988– | Fathers and sons—United
States—Biography. | Football players—United States—Biography. |
Rugby football players—United States—Biography. |
Olympic athletes—United States—Biography.
Classification: LCC GV939.E27 A3 2021 (print) | LCC GV939.E27
(ebook) | DDC 796.33092 [B]–dc23
LC record available at https://lccn.loc.gov/2020028103
LC ebook record available at https://lccn.loc.gov/2020028104

Printed in the United States of America
1st Printing

DESIGNED BY MEIGHAN CAVANAUGH

Contents

Foreword

I was named the head football coach at the Ohio State University in December 2011, and I immediately started to evaluate the entire program, staff, and players. Having just lost to their hated rival, the Buckeyes were preparing to play Florida in the Gator Bowl. Watching game videos of the entire season, I focused on each player, looking for tough, selfless individuals who played with relentless effort and energy. I believe that the special teams players, and their play in particular, are the window into the heart of the entire team. After hours of evaluation, I found myself a fan of one particular player, number 34.

Upon checking the roster, I was heartbroken to find that number 34 was a senior. Coach Luke Fickell told me that Nate Ebner was a former OSU rugby player who walked on to the football team and became the heart and soul of the Buckeyes' special teams. This confirmed what I already knew and reaffirmed why I became a college football coach. Football is the consummate *team* sport, and special teams and its players average close to forty plays per game and totally embrace the "team first" ethos, a selfless attitude and esprit de corps. Nate Ebner is the type of player who would jump off the screen when I watched game films every Sunday to get a picture of our next opponent. If their special teams lacked energy and were not in sync, I knew that their staff and team could not control our final score on Saturday. However, if they were inspired, well coached, played hard and fast, and had elite players like Nate Ebner, I knew we would be in the fight of fights.

Meeting Nate Ebner following the Gator Bowl in January only confirmed his elite status. Not surprisingly, I met him in the Buckeyes' weight room. We would meet a number of times over the next few years as he returned to train in Columbus, and I started to learn the story of his unique journey. He began his *athletic* journey in earnest as an elite rugby player, then a walk-on OSU football player, to OSU football captain and scholarship player, to an NFL career with the New England Patriots, to multiple Super Bowl victories, and back to rugby as an Olympian. Nate kept pursuing his dreams even when he had to step backward at times to do it. As he says here, "Nothing is more motivating or crazy or holds more chances for glory or disaster than something done for love."

Love is the real subject here. Nate Ebner's story as both son and athlete is, from the beginning, inspired by the power of his parents' love. The Ebners were a family separated by divorce, yet kept together by a mother and father devoted to putting their children first. The power of love is crystal clear here: Jeff Ebner instilled in Nate his values by building a father-and-son relationship nurtured by tough love, hard work, high expectations, and loving encouragement to achieve. Their relationship was built on that rock, and it survived even after Jeff's tragic death, as his spirit endured during the difficult decisions and physical ordeals that were to come for Nate. I've been honored to coach very few athletes who God blessed to know and experience the power of inspiration based on love and ownership. They disregard pain, discomfort, and injury with a mental toughness that pushes the mind and body beyond its perceived limits. This was Nate's edge. His inspiration was much greater than "motivation." While motivation is also powerful, it wanes as its energy, which is sourced from a combination of love, hate, and fear, is drained during competition.

This book should be a mandatory read. Parents: This is a read about how to spell "love" . . . T-I-M-E. It's about a father who devoted time to his son . . . quality time. It is about a mother who came to her son's rescue when his father was tragically murdered. Coaches: Read the details of the value of creating an elite organization and the impact it has on players . . . Jim Tressel, Bill Belichick, and Mike Friday. We are the foundation of Nate's journey. Athletes: This is a testimony to the timeless truth that is overlooked today . . . Greatness is *hard*! There are no shortcuts, hangers-on, or social media platforms that lead one to greatness. Not even hard work itself will lead to greatness. Only the relentless pursuit of a vision, a never-quit-and-refuse-to-lose mentality, and, finally, the embrace of the discomfort and pain associated with greatness, will suffice. In the words of Nate and his dad, "Conquer the pain and the glory will last forever."

I knew this book would be elite and I was not disappointed. It is even more. Having a dream is great, but working at whatever level is necessary to reach it is a necessity. Achieving that dream is transformational.

URBAN MEYER

Over Our Skis

I t was an insane place for a couple novice skiers from Ohio to be.

Highland Bowl rises like a vision of dread from the necklace of two-mile-high peaks surrounding Aspen, Colorado. Its slope angle reaches 48 degrees at the summit, 12,392 feet above sea level, where my dad and I should have been if we'd had less attitude and more sense. I was twelve and thought I was immortal. My dad, Jeff Ebner, was forty-six and knew he was.

That morning, we'd briefly discussed our desire to check out Highland Bowl. We'd taken ski trips out west before, to Colorado and Utah. We knew what we knew. Which wasn't a lot, as it turned out. That didn't deter us. Jeff Ebner had a wayward, cocksure confidence that discouraged all doubts. It applied to everything he did. I was born with some of it. By the time we studied Highland Bowl, I'd learned the rest. My dad's confidence made me believe we could do anything.

His logic was admirably consistent: *If other people can do it, why can't we? Someone knows how to fix this car engine, why can't I? Let me get the manual. Others are working hard to realize their unlikely dreams. Why shouldn't we?*

My dad sized up the crew of people we'd joined on the ski lift. He said, "If all these old, unathletic, overweight people who have never lifted a weight in their lives can do it, why can't we?" He didn't offer this in a bragging way. My dad was confident, not a braggart. There was a difference.

Given that we were, in fact, stronger and younger than the others in the group and that we were, for sure, workout obsessives who'd already run halfway up a mountain earlier that day, even before we pulled on our ski boots, Jeff Ebner's logic seemed unassailable to me.

"You wanna do it?" I asked.

"You only live once," my dad said.

There's no true manual for living. You can seek out advice from a book, but often that advice comes from someone who never got it right himself. There's a lot to be said for specialized knowledge, but on some level if you need to read about how to be a good parent, you're probably not going to be one. If you gotta ask, you'll never know.

My dad was a simple guy, who valued obvious truths and squeezed them for every drop of living they contained. You want to be a good father? Time and love. "You spell love T-I-M-E," he'd say. Nothing else is so concrete. Not saying the perfect thing, not buying the perfect gift or smothering your child with affection that's not always real, or really wanted. Not trying to handle every situation properly. No one gets that right every time. Relationships involve some stumbling in the dark. Only time and love are enduring and authentic.

Our love was quirky, because Jeff Ebner was the quirkiest man most men had ever met. He died at fifty-three, too young for someone so full of the world. Maybe he knew tragedy was coming and compensated for it by giving his life a workout it would not forget. Or maybe he never gave mortality a passing thought.

Highland Bowl was the backdrop for the 1993 movie *Aspen Extreme*. It was prone to avalanches, a fact our driver casually mentioned as he escorted us to the summit. We'd ridden the lift most of the way up. A guy driving a tractor would get us the rest of the way to the top. "This is some of the most extreme skiing you can find in North America," he said over the loudspeaker.

I gulped. Did my dad? I'm thinking, hell yeah, he did. He didn't want me to see his concern. He didn't want me to think we were so far over our skis on this one, we'd have to fall backward to stand up straight. "We got this," was all he said.

I never wanted to let my dad down, and I didn't back off from challenges. For at least five years, we'd worked out together, run hills together, found new roads to bicycle. He was crazy about rugby, so we spent weekends at practice together. He ran an auto salvage yard, so I got good at pulling parts from dead cars. He and my mother divorced when I was a toddler. That didn't curtail my dad's devotion to me. If anything, it enhanced it and enforced it.

If he did it, I did it. We moved mountains. Literally and figuratively. You try loading a crushed junker into the back of a semitruck. Everything we did together served as a time-love lesson on how I could become a better person. He was my dad. I was his Why.

Years later, after his death, the roles reversed. Jeff Ebner would become my Why. Love and time would still be shared. Even if apart. Somehow. I'd dedicate myself to honoring his memory. Everything I'd do on the football field, on the rugby pitch, and, eventually, in my life as a husband—and someday I trust as a father—would reflect the love and time I shared with my dad.

In the meantime, there we were, staring across this ten- or fifteen-foot crevasse we had to leap across, just to reach the beginning of the ski run from hell.

My dad had always given me the security that things would work out, and the confidence to make that so. Let's do this.

I should say that no sensible person with our limited experience would even consider skiing the Highland Bowl. We crept to the edge of the slope, which looked more like a cliff. We made the leap across the ditch.

I can see my dad now, in his goofy goggles and thirty-year-old ski suit, telling me how we were going to tame this mountain, as the old, unathletic people who'd never lifted a weight in their pathetic lives bombed down the hill past us, like pros.

The plan was to ski sideways down the mountain, zigzagging parallel to the slope until we approached the bottom. If we started going out-of-control fast, we'd purposely turn straight into the mountain and fall down. We did all that, until we reached a turn onto a path that would take us around the mountain, to the "normal slopes" where we should have been in the first place.

Jeff Ebner missed the turn and, with no control at all, flew off the slope and into a stand of pines. I freaked out, thinking he was hurt. As I lumbered across the slope in my dad's general direction, I heard his creepy little laugh from the base of a pine.

"Heh heh heh," he said. "That wasn't so bad."

Life, I learned, would be trial and error. The error would always be forgiven. The effort, the trial, had to be made, and it had to be made honestly and with the fullest intent. Often, I'd enter into something with a naivete that would have been reckless had I not been consumed by the need to succeed. In a way, the wacky run down Highland Bowl was no different than walking onto the football team at Ohio State or being drafted into the NFL or marching into Maracanã Stadium at the 2016 Olympics. Each was an improbable dream. The Jeff Ebner alchemy of blind faith and hard work saw me through. We could have walked away from that mountain. We got our asses up and we got our asses down.

When I talk about my dad now, two decades removed from Highland Bowl, people want to know how we created such a relationship. As if there were some step-by-step plan. There wasn't.

It was just two people who shared the same joys in life. We liked each other's company. And then he died, leaving me empty and full at the same time. Empty with the sadness that comes from losing my best friend. Full with the purpose of a promise made. You can miss someone while also feeling his presence. Your little wins can be his, in his absence. But not without an excruciating pain that can make you feel most alive, while sometimes wishing you weren't.

After my parents split up, I watched my dad make two-hour round trips three or four times a week, from Springfield, Ohio, to my mom's house in Mason, just to share a meal with me. He was there whenever my car needed fixing. He flew solo to Wales to watch me play rugby in the Junior World Cup. I'd call him every day, even if just to tell him the workout numbers I'd put up. I made that call on the day he died. We shared anything and everything. He never thought twice about doing anything, if it was for me. The memories of the trips we took are family heirlooms now, no different to me than a photo album or a grandmother's diamond-crusted wedding band.

Some people have a showy way of displaying their affections. That's fine. I don't trust it, though. It seems staged. My dad and I expressed our love frequently, but quietly and without show. We weren't big on "I love yous" on the phone or buying gifts for each other at the appropriate times. He'd say those gestures were "a given." When your actions are genuine expressions of love, your words don't need a stage.

I miss him terribly, but I try not to dwell on that. Dwelling does no one any good. It's a waste of energy. He wouldn't want me to do it. I've tried to remember that at the important moments in my life when I wished he was there.

We had an ethos, a path, whatever you want to call it. We were on it, and the only thing we didn't do was deviate from it. And so we stood on that ledge at Highland Bowl, where we had no business being, and we jumped off.

In November 2008, I delivered the eulogy at my dad's funeral. I told the story of Highland Bowl, and I finished with this:

"I hope if I ever become a father that I can be half the man to my son that he was to me. And to show the love he showed, which was genuine and real. A favorite quote of his that he used only when necessary—usually while we were doing some of our crazy workouts—was, 'Only the great ones can deal with the pain. I know it hurts, but can you fight through it is the question. A-ight, Eb. Let's see what you got. Finish strong.'"

I've dealt with the pain of losing my dad by living a life he'd be proud of. One of these days I'll go back to Highland Bowl, hopefully with a son or daughter of my own. We'll share the heirloom.

My dad's short life was a raucous novel, notable for its well-lived moments, not for the number of pages turned. He finished strong. As for the both of us?

We lived, man. We lived.

Finish Strong

ONE

Cowards Can't Tackle

My dad was a rugby goon. They all were.

They were regular guys. Salesmen and tradesmen, construction workers, and one particular auto salvage man, whose idea of rugby subtlety was a shot to the sternum. They showed up on weekends ready to smash opponents on the pitch, then drink beer with them afterward. American rugby was not the elegantly brutish game the rest of the world played. Not even by 2001, when I played in my first game. It was middle-aged men, mugging one another for kicks, before limping off to the post-match party. America's rugby cliché had a home in Columbus, Ohio, with the Scioto Valley Rugby Club.

As my dad put it, "Where else can you beat the shit out of people for a couple hours and not go to jail?"

Who else would gladly dig deep into his own pockets to play a game with intangible rewards? It was about winning, sure, but define *winning*. A place in the national championship tournament is nice. Is it as satisfying as road-trip weekends with people you enjoy and a game you literally ache to play? What's the going rate for good memories?

Jeff and his mates showed up on weekends at tournaments all over the Midwest. Former high school and college football players and college club ruggers arrived in a caravan of vehicles on a Friday night, bunking four to a room in a low-cost hotel or motel. Most were at least a decade removed from their undergraduate or post-high-school glory. You didn't have to be skilled to call yourself a rugby player. You didn't have to be experienced, either. Rugby has always been a game best learned on the pitch. You just needed a high pain tolerance and an affection for hitting people.

My father took the stress of Monday through Friday and shared it with his opponents on Saturday. They'd feel it in their ribs. You didn't have to run an auto salvage yard, as my dad did, to understand this singular satisfaction. But it helped.

He was a workout obsessive, strong and tireless. But he wasn't that big (five foot nine) and he didn't weigh a lot (180 pounds). His teammates called him "The Cannonball." No one gasped at his speed, and his skills weren't remarkable. When I was fourteen, I was already technically a better player than he was. But my dad was a tough son of a bitch. "Ebs would knock your dick in the dirt," was how his friend and Scioto Valley coach Steve Finkel described him.

Jeff Ebner was fearless. He was, in fact, a little beyond fearless. On the pitch, my dad could be a little . . . off. You can't play rugby well at any level if you play scared. My dad routinely squared up against guys well over six feet and way beyond two hundred pounds. I never saw him miss a tackle. One of the first things he said to me about rugby was, "Cowards can't tackle." I couldn't have been more than ten.

He played center for Scioto Valley, and he measured his success by the number of big hits he administered. "Smashes," in rugby parlance. "You get your smashes in, Ebs?" Finkel wanted to know, after every match. It was a rhetorical question.

There was more to club rugby than weekend warriors rekindling their youth while partying like frat brothers. Respectful civility lived beneath the game's violence. Rugby is generous with the nobility it bestows on everyone who plays it for any length of time. After smashing a guy in the afternoon, you'd be sharing stories with him at night.

My dad appreciated the rugby ethos: Respect everyone, get your smashes in, leave it on the field. Play for love, because there is no money, a fact that only enhances the game's nobility. Play through pain, because you're going to get hurt. Not seriously, usually. You're not allowed to hit anybody above the shoulders. But enough pain that you'd feel it a few days afterward. Kind of a three-Advil ache. Play for each other.

My dad admired the selflessness the best teams had. It was a team game. Rugby players work hard, mainly because running and tackling and running some more are hard labor. You can't be out of shape.

Rugby asks for a certain humility. It's an egalitarian game. No player is above another. Each is a link in the chain of the team. If everyone doesn't work together, the whole thing falls apart. Plus, no one who is tackled twenty times a game can feel entitled. Or immortal. Everyone wears the same dirt.

Jeff Ebner never thought he was a cut above. His friend Mike Garcia once described my dad as "the slag from the melting pot." My dad stayed true to who he was. He was secure enough in his own skin to believe that was plenty good enough, on and off the pitch.

From the time I was six, I'd tag along with him to his games and practices. Why? My dad loved rugby. I loved my dad. Big relationships really can be that simple. He said this, in a speech the day they inducted him into the Scioto Valley Rugby Club's Hall of Fame:

"Many, many years ago, rugby became the marrow of my life, a mistress I couldn't get rid of. The dirt, the grass, the sweat are smells and tastes forever etched in my mind. The game made me who I am today."

He drove a blue diesel pickup truck, with our retriever dog, Magnum, in the bed. He'd get to practice, chain Magnum to a pole, then get naked in the parking lot while changing into his practice gear. The fact there might be women practicing close by didn't bother my dad. He wasn't hung up on appearances. "It's fine," he'd say.

I carried the water jug, a gallon plastic container, its outside so filthy from use at the junkyard, his teammates never drank from it.

I saw my dad in practice fight guys he'd known for twenty years, after he'd smashed them in what were supposed to be games of one-hand touch. I watched him slop Red Hot all over his legs and shoulders before games to ease the pain from some stray injury he'd incurred at the junkyard or while gloriously abusing his body in the name of smashes. He once pulled both hamstrings in a single game. No problem. Red Hot, sleeve, good to go.

The problem with the Red Hot was, even if he covered the analgesic goop in a sleeve, it would leak. Other guys would partake, involuntarily. Red Hot is exactly as its name implies. Ground chili peppers was its only ingredient. Guys with fair skin actually got blisters from the stuff. My dad's logic, which he shared with the burn victims, was simple:

"If the Red Hot burns more than the pain, you're good."

More than a decade later, I was a New England Patriot playing with a pulled groin. At halftime of a game against the Indianapolis Colts, our trainer, Joe Van Allen, slapped some Atomic Balm on my groin. Just writing that sentence makes me wince. Atomic Balm is a step cooler than Red Hot. Even so, my leg was burning off. Van Allen suggested we cut off the wrap, wipe off some of the Atomic Balm, and rewrap it. I refused, even as my leg felt flame broiled.

"My dad, if he were in a grave, would roll over. He would die again," I said. I played the rest of the game with that shit burning a hole in my leg.

I watched the Scioto Valley games on weekends, Ebs getting his smashes in, knocking dicks in the dirt. I played touch before the games, with other kids. By the time I was twelve, I was bringing my kit (jersey, shorts, shoes), in case the men ever needed an emergency fill-in. I always wondered what it'd be like to knock someone's junk in the dirt. I was thirteen when it first happened.

"Go play on the wing," my dad said. That's where all the newbies played. On the wing.

It was a B-side game in Dayton, Ohio. I was five foot six and 120 pounds. If I hadn't had my jersey tucked into my shorts, it would have been dancing at my knees. Was I ready? Did it matter?

My dad's niche was toughness. He tackled well, because tackling was a test of manhood, and he didn't flunk those tests. Technique wasn't essential in club rugby; want-to was. But this was crazy. What other contact sport has thirteen-year-olds playing against grown men? There weren't youth rugby leagues in the US at the time. If I wanted to play in a game, I had no choice. So there I was, out on the wing, reciting my dad's mantra in my head . . . *cowards can't tackle, cowards can't tackle.*

This wasn't simply about bringing down the guy across from me. To my dad, tackling was a metaphor for everything he did. He tackled his work (sometimes literally, when thieves invaded the junkyard); he tackled his workouts, keeping notes on every lift, run, and personal best; he tackled his duties as a father, raising me with devotion. Tackling was essential to who he was. That made it essential to me.

Mark the man across from me. Run the ball if I get it, get in the breakdown if someone near me gets tackled. Then . . .

The guy had to be a solid 220 pounds. He had the ball. He wasn't close to me. He was running right at me, in space. He was gonna baptize this kid playing a man's game.

Who was I going to be?

That guy who shies from contact and eventually gets his head taken off? Or the guy who isn't a coward? "How you respond to that situation says a lot about you," Jeff Ebner said, often. Now, Jeff Ebner was at my side, in a game.

I'd played peewee football. I'd practiced with the men. I knew how to tackle. It was a mindset. It was a metaphor for everything my father was and wanted me to be.

The guy charged me. He tried to get low. I put my head to the side, stepped in with my right leg and shoulder, grabbed him by the ankles and held on. He dropped like a chopped tree. *I'm not a coward,* I said to myself.

I've played a lot of rugby since then: Scioto Valley, club ball at Ohio State, US national teams, the Olympic team in 2016. I've tackled more people than I can recall. Rugby players, football players, petty thieves at the junkyard. That instant has never left me. Jeff Ebner rarely missed a tackle. In the two decades since, I've worked hard to have the same thing said of me.

Rugby was my dad's passion and the clearest reflection of who he was. It was our connective tissue, the living bridge between who Jeff Ebner was and who he wanted me to be. I would go on to make a living playing football, earning three Super Bowl rings, All-Pro honors, and a lifetime of memories. At heart, I've always been a rugby guy playing football. I was my father's son. I wasn't a coward. I made the tackle.

"Great job, Eb," Jeff Ebner said to me on the drive home.

TWO

My Father's Son

When I was two years old, I carried my tricycle up the stairs of our house and rode it down. My mother gasped. My dad applauded my coordination.

I was a hyper little kid. When I was four and couldn't sleep, my dad would say, "Show me how fast you can run around the house" to wear me out. When I was six, I watched my dad lift weights in the medieval-looking room behind our detached garage. He handed me a broomstick and showed me proper bench-pressing form.

I wasn't mischievous. Most of the stuff I did that might be considered mischievous—that is, just about everything I did at the junkyard—was perfectly acceptable junkyard activity. Smashing car windows with baseball bats was OK in my world.

Mainly, I respected Jeff Ebner. I never wanted to disappoint him. I wanted him to feel as good about me as I did about him.

I could be tempted, though. I could be swayed into doing unacceptable things.

I was twelve or thirteen when Matt Koman and I used my slingshot to launch rocks and acorns at passing cars. Matt had come up from Mason for the day, to my dad's house on High Street. We ended up in the tree house in the backyard, seeing if our projectiles could reach High Street out front. They couldn't, so we moved up and hid behind a bush in the corner of the front yard.

There was no shortage of traffic on High Street, a major two-lane that passes through Springfield. We hit four or five vehicles, including a truck, whose driver wasn't happy. He slammed on his brakes, we ran into the house. The guy came to the front door.

"Gimme the slingshot," he said. We did.

The guy knew my dad and somehow knew this was his house. He took the slingshot to the junkyard and showed Jeff Ebner the dent in his truck. Matt and I were in the weight room behind the garage when my dad walked in. He was calm, which was far scarier than if he'd just started screaming at us, because my dad never screamed. He spoke in measured tones, like a judge ordering a defendant to the electric chair. "Matt, I'm not your dad, so I'm not going to punish you," he said. "I am going to punish Nate."

Since I'd never before transgressed to quite that extent, I didn't know what to expect. My dad had never laid a hand on me. Never so much as raised his voice at me. But this . . . oh, man. This was unexplored territory.

My dad went to the house. He came back with a pair of safety scissors. The kind you might use in kindergarten. Short, with its points rounded at the end. "Go cut the grass," he said to me.

I looked at Matt. Matt looked at me.

"What?" I said.

Jeff Ebner ordered me to cut the backyard with the safety scissors. He would watch, he said, to make sure I did it right. At that point, I didn't know quite what to do. It was comical, but I didn't dare so much as grin. It was ridiculous, for obvious reasons, but I didn't risk questioning him. If this were to be my punishment for purposely denting a truck with a rock, well, cool.

I spent the next two hours on my hands and knees trimming individual blades of grass with a six-year-old's scissors. When my dad felt enough grass had been sufficiently barbered, he said, "Grab your cleats, we're going to the water tower." Springfield's water tower rested atop one of the town's nastiest hills. It was one of the hills we ran for our workouts. He watched as I ran ten sprints up and down the hill.

That was the kind of relationship we had. My dad knew I wasn't a bad kid. He knew that I knew I'd messed up and felt bad about it. The grass trimming was pointless and boring because he knew that even at age twelve, I hated pointless and boring. It was like moving rocks from one pile to another. The running would serve two masters. It would punish me for what

I'd done, but also help my conditioning. He'd never simply send me to my room to stare at the walls.

Jeff Ebner had a problem with parents who yelled at their kids in public, especially at practice or a game. I had a youth baseball coach like that. After one screaming jag, my dad told the coach, "You ever yell at my kid like that, we're going to have a problem."

Because of how my dad was, no coach has ever motivated me with yelling or constant criticism. Negativity doesn't work with me.

My dad was an intimidating dude. That alone helped to keep me in line. I'd seen him with the robbers at the yard. But he was reasonable with the justice he meted out, and he wasn't immune to admitting a mistake. He coached my high school rugby team, and he could get a little vociferous, especially with me. He was on me once during a game, when I'd had enough.

"Shut up!" I yelled at him, on the fly.

That prompted a visit from my dad, on the field, during the game. "I'm your dad!" he said. "You can't talk to me like that."

I agreed. "You're right, I shouldn't do that. But you shouldn't be out here."

"Yeah, you're right," he said, retreating to the sideline. And that was that.

Back to my rock-slinging incident. My dad called the driver of the dented truck and agreed to pay for the damages. I never slung a rock at a moving vehicle again. Or tried to mow the lawn with a pair of scissors.

I was the fourteen-year-old working summers at Ebner's Auto Parts, pulling catalytic converters from cars and learning the only reasonable way to deal with robbers. (It didn't involve calling the cops.) Before I played a minute of club rugby or college football, I knew how to bring a man down.

WHEN I WAS THE sixteen-year-old on the cusp of a career as a US national rugby player, my dad was finding new hills for us to run in Springfield. And I do mean us. Jeff Ebner did everything he ever asked me to do. My dad's spirit never aged. He noted our progress in little black books, not only to make me feel good about the work I was putting in and the growth that came from it, but also to hammer home lessons. To him, everything came with a lesson, and his lessons were basic:

Work hard, finish strong, never quit. Push through the pain. Own it and enjoy it as a symbol of overcoming and winning. Set goals, make commitments, honor them. Relish the little wins.

These are clichés, of course, But their timelessness should never be shrugged away. My dad never did anything without a purpose. He loved competition. He knew he could use it to help me navigate life.

You can have anything if you're willing to sacrifice everything. I live by that maxim.

It's who I am. I owe that to my dad. It all started in a room full of clouds.

THREE

Working Out

When I was six, I was hanging upside down from old-school inversion boots attached to a chin-up bar, watching my dad bench-press two hundred pounds of unadorned metal plates. It was winter in Ohio and freezing outside, but in here, in this room behind the detached garage of our house on High Street, it was so warm the walls were sweating.

Jeff Ebner had installed a heater and hooked it to a propane tank he brought home from the junkyard. He'd turn it on thirty minutes before working out. The thing was so loud, you could hear it from inside the house. Whenever Jeff cranked up the heater, my stepmother, Amy, would go for a walk. It was fine.

The room sweated as much as we did. Condensation formed on every metal object and surface. The weight bars got slick. To fix that, my dad had brick-sized blocks of chalk. We covered our hands and shoulders in the stuff. Even the bar got a veneer of chalk. "Chalk up, Ebs," Jeff would order. Chalk clouds coated the room in ghostly white, like a bad L.A. smog. When the chalk flew, work got done.

At first, chalking up was fun. I was working out, just like my dad. As I got older, the chalk would signify serious intent. Extra sets, more reps, heavy loads. *Time to get busy, Ebs. Chalk up.*

Jeff Ebner was thirty-nine when I was six. He looked it, from the neck up. His hairline had begun to retreat. His face was already assuming a handsome cragginess, incipient lines forming from the ups and downs of his life. The rest of him looked ageless.

He didn't lift to make the shirts fit better. The room didn't have a mirror. It didn't feature nice benches or a wall full of big TVs. Lifting was serious business, the weight room primal and basic, everything included but charm. Maybe its dungeon chic was its charm. The workout room was a shrine to Jeff Ebner's duct-tape ingenuity and his It's Fine sensibilities.

To him, working out was relatable to everything essential in life. Setting goals, reaching them. Honoring commitments. Being accountable. You start, you finish. You finish strong. This was his mentality. Working hard is a skill. Practice it enough, it can be second nature. Working out was a demonstration of who my dad was. And who he'd like me to be.

The weights and the machines were a mishmash of dependable junk and as such, a decent representation of what my dad knew to be important. Substance over style, sleeveless and raw. No bullshit or Spandex. Here's a dumbbell. Curl it. A weight was a weight.

The walls were unfinished, the business ends of rusted nails poking into the room. Watch yourself. If you walked down the center of the room, past the bench press, there was a back door that led to a kennel and a doghouse filled with hay, for whichever massive mutt we owned at the time.

Over here, a weight bench, its brown fake leather cut and pasted with duct tape, which was my father's solution to any household problem. Over there, a leg press machine, its seat covered in ruby-red fake leather and more duct tape. Hunks of puke-yellow carpet in places my dad felt needed extra padding. In between, a bunch of jury-rigged machines, benches and weight stands, set atop a concrete floor softened here and there with carpet remnants, where he'd drop three hundred pounds of weights during a powerlifting session.

Jeff Ebner was the duct-tape king. If there were a duct-tape championship of the world, he'd be holding the title belt over his head. Duct-taped to his fingers, so no one could pry it away.

Duct tape was suited to any Fuck It problem he had. It was strong. It was effective, it lasted, it was cheap. It was fine. Even better, duct tape looked like, well, like duct tape. It was my dad.

Very few everyday fixes could not be made with duct tape. Duct tape on the water hose at the junkyard, after the glass and steel on the ground had sliced the hose to ribbons. It was that or buy a new hose every other week. We'd never do that.

Duct tape in the weight room, naturally, Band-Aiding every bench and mat. We weren't there to impress anyone. Duct tape for the torn seat of our Jet Ski. That one was especially effective because when you sat on the Jet Ski, the tape was invisible. Duct tape on his sneakers, when their soles ripped apart. Which they did, invariably, possibly because my dad bought them at closeout sales.

He didn't use it on everything. Matters of safety were not given the duct tape once-over. Not even Jeff Ebner would duct-tape a forty-thousand-pound front loader or a family vehicle. At that point, he'd apply his intense focus and stubbornness, often with the help of the piles of repair manuals he kept on hand.

Part of it was pride. "If someone else can fix it, why can't I? I've got books on plumbing," he reasoned. Part of it was the challenge. The more frustrating the fix, the more determined he'd become.

He'd obsess over fixing a car engine rather than pay someone to fix it. "You know how much they'd charge me for that?" We had several Mercedes as I was growing up. My dad would buy them at auctions in Columbus and occasionally in Florida. Whenever a Mercedes or any vehicle we owned needed to be fixed, he'd pull out his stash of paperback repair manuals. My grandfather Dick owned a BMW, I had a Ford. A battalion of Caterpillars lived at the junkyard. "This engine isn't smarter than me," Dad would say.

Jeff Ebner would take an engine apart, make what he thought was the needed repair, put it back together, and if it still didn't work (which was often the case), he'd take it apart again.

That's why a lot of our stuff was jury-rigged. Anything that required welding, he welded it. The only repairs he hated doing were to things around the house. "I fix stuff all day" at the junkyard, he reasoned. Everything else—plumbing, engine repair, construction jobs (the infamous deck you'll soon read about, the second-floor office at the yard), dumbbells, weight-lifting machines—attracted my dad's (devout) attention and (questionable) skills.

I recall my dad and I painting an old beater truck. With paintbrushes. And house paint.

It all came back to his core values. If the job were important for safety or functionality, or there was a good chance a tape job wouldn't hold, he'd switch up. Otherwise, duct tape. It was a metaphor for how he looked at the world. Anything could be fixed, and he would do the fixing.

Somebody knew how to fix this stuff, right? They're not smarter than I am.

My dad was frugal, but he was also someone who didn't need a lot of pricey comforts. When I say he was simple, I don't mean he wasn't educated or curious. He was content. He had his rugby, his son, his yard, and his girl. That was all he needed. None of it could be improved upon by spending lots of money.

I drove our 1988 S-class on my first date with Chelsey, the woman who would become my wife. It was older than I was, a turbo diesel without the turbo. Getting on a highway was life-endangering. I'd jam the gas pedal to the floor, the S-class would lurch like an elevator stuck between floors. I wasn't late to the date, but only because I'm never late. I gave myself five or ten extra minutes. I never asked Chelsey what she thought of the car.

When my dad was feeling especially conservative, he wouldn't drive a Mercedes or a pickup truck to rugby practice. It was an eighty-mile round trip and great gas mileage was not a strength of either car or truck, so Jeff Ebner drove his Vespa on back roads. Not even my dad took that thing on the highway. It got 80 miles per gallon, though.

Clothes didn't impress him. On rugby road trips, he'd wear his dress blues from work and bring along a sport coat, on the off chance he'd need one to get into a restaurant. Picture a guy wearing a sport coat over a workingman's shirt and pants. That was him.

Occasionally, he and Amy would go through his closet. "Ames, time for a purge," he'd say. It wasn't always easy for the man who duct-taped his gym shoes. "I could get a couple more wears outta that," he'd protest. "Trash," Amy would reply, pointing to the garbage can. That said, I don't know if she ever convinced him to part with the brown corduroy suit from the 1970s.

He wasn't Scrooge, though. The point was more about pride and contentment than squeezing Benjamins. As a junkyard proprietor, my dad was more concerned with how things worked than what they looked like.

He splurged on vacations. He never said a trip was too costly or a restaurant too expensive. The only special item he ever bought for himself was a video camera, so he could shoot my rugby matches.

He bought Amy lots of jewelry. "Do you like it?" he'd ask.

"Yeah. But I don't need it."

"Do you like it?"

"Yes, but . . ."

"We'll take it."

Our squat rack had no conventional means of holding the weight bar. We used car jacks, one on each end of the bench, to maneuver the bar up or down. Picture lifting a car to change a tire. That's how we adjusted the height of the weights.

The jacks rested on top of a four-inch-thick rubber platform, covered by more puke-yellow carpet. It was functional and ridiculous. You would look at the whole setup and ask, "What the fuck is that?"

My dad's answer was always, "Can you do the exercise?"

"Yes."

"OK, then it's fine." It's Fine was his favorite expression. It's Fine was versatile and practical and dismissed all he saw as trivial, which was just about everything. It was duct tape in words. *If it'll do, if it works, go with it. It's fine.*

The weights, too, were pure It's Fine. Steve Finkel owned a welding business, so he had access to metal-cutting tools. My dad would say to Finkel, "Give me a hundred-pound piece of metal and put a hole in the middle. It needs to be this thick and this much in diameter." The plates were blank and smooth, no writing on them, no cutouts. Just big, dense plates. For dumbbells, my dad used pieces of railroad ties cut from the abandoned tracks that ran behind Ebner's. He welded almost-circular globs of metal to each end. It was medieval.

My dad was picky about his barbells, though. They got used more than anything else in a workout, so he wanted them the way he wanted them. He'd go to closeout sales at gyms, to buy York bars. Only York, without a lot of heavy knurling, the serrated grip, at the ends. He liked the bars smooth. They didn't rip up his hands.

He wrote every workout detail in his little black book. He'd script our sessions before we started, down to the type of exercise, the number of reps and sets we'd do, and the pieces of equipment we'd use. The hills we'd run, the times we expected, the splits we'd record, five hundred meters at a time, on the rowing machine. It was meticulous. It gave us a measure, over time, of how we were doing and who we were. Accountable people do what they say they'll do.

It gave us an accurate reading we could adjust upward in the days and weeks that followed. The black book notes had another aim: to show me what I could achieve when I put in the work. The black book was the daily diary of our earnest intentions. *This is how far we've come. This is where we're going.* It was the Bible then. Now, a few decades later, it survives in my memory as a forever reminder of the need to follow through. When I commit publicly to doing something, I don't quit on it.

We competed, because competing was fun. Away from work, Jeff Ebner didn't do much that wasn't fun. Chin-ups, push-ups, sit-ups. He'd attach a forty-five-pound weight to his belt and say, "I can still do more dips than you." Or, "How many crunches can you do, Nate? Not enough to beat me."

As I moved into my teenage years, I really wanted to beat my dad. He'd trick me into thinking I was close, whether it was crunches, push-ups, bench presses, basketball, squash, rowing, anything. He'd always do one more rep than I could do, pretending to agonize over that last rep, to make it dramatic for my benefit. "Still family champ," he'd say. We'd play squash and he'd let me get just close enough to believe I would win, then "magically" rally to beat me.

At this point, maybe you're thinking, *This is heavy-duty regimentation for a kid.*

You'd be right. The difference was, I loved it all. It was never a job, maybe because my dad was never anything but positive about what we were doing. "You got this, Nate. Good job, Nate. Look at how much more you're lifting than last year. Look how fast you are, how high you jump." Later on, first at Ohio State and then in the NFL with the New England Patriots, the approach was less positive. That only made me more grateful for Jeff Ebner's ways.

He was no helicopter parent. Our lives became inextricable, especially the older I became, but my dad didn't live vicariously through me. Unlike some parents (and coaches), Jeff never cracked the proverbial whip, never belittled me. That stuff didn't get my attention. Telling me how bad I was didn't motivate me to be good. The workouts were hard enough without that.

He'd say, "Keep fighting, Ebs. You're a beast." Not, "Don't even try, Ebs, you'll never be able to do it, anyway." There was a world of difference in his approach, compared with the tactics used by lots of youth coaches who believed they were Vince Lombardi. My dad told me I was a beast. After a while, I believed I was.

He saw the weight room as a classroom, and me as his only pupil. He insisted I finish what I started, that I didn't give in to myself. But he never forced me to do something I didn't want to do. And he did it all with me.

He saw my potential and he didn't let me rest until I reached it. Then he'd simply scribble in the little black book and reset the bar. "You have to want your body to be something it's not," he'd say. "You devote yourself to that every single day."

I felt good about the little wins. Five pounds more on the bench press, grinding through an extra set of dumbbell flys. This pushing through—and seeing positive outcomes—was what made me believe. And want more.

As I got older and things got serious, he'd add this: "If you can suffer through the pain, the glory will last forever." I never leaned on those words more than when I was grinding my way through the agony of pre-Olympic rugby workouts, in 2016. I heard them the night I walked into Maracanã Stadium in Rio de Janeiro, as a member of the US Olympic team.

By my early teens, I was realizing the essential and honest truths of working out: I reaped what I sowed. Achievement came with effort. When it came to effort, I was completely in control. If I worked hard enough, I could create the changes I wanted. I could control the outcome. I liked that.

We'd take to the roads and run. Penn Street, Willow Road, the water tower, the steps of the football stadium at Wittenberg College. Never less than forty-five-degree inclines. When we'd run out of new hills to conquer, Jeff Ebner would drive around Springfield, seeking other ones to put in the black book. "Let it rip, Nate, I'm right behind you!"

Nothing kept us from the grind. My dad loved the grind. The mental steel it forged, the accountability, the confidence. In the winter when it snowed and we needed to get in a run on the middle-school track, we'd shovel the two inside lanes, wearing surgical masks so our lungs wouldn't frost.

When I was little we did the backyard Olympics. Weight lifting, running, jumping. Jeff would note scrupulously my gains from year to year. I worked hard. I saw improvement. It was all fun to me. That was one of my dad's gifts. He got me to love working out. By the time I was sixteen or so, it wasn't just something I enjoyed. It was a lifestyle.

I didn't know it then, but what we were doing in our little gym of chalk clouds and contraptions would set me up for life. Jeff Ebner wasn't just building my muscles. Very deliberately and with a subtlety a child could never detect, my dad was building my mind. To him, body and mind were parts of the same machine.

Training properly and with purpose demanded accountability. I couldn't not show up. When I showed up, I couldn't not commit fully, and I damned sure couldn't quit. My dad didn't let me walk away from things I didn't like or things that weren't going well. I was allowed to be fatigued. I wasn't allowed to use fatigue as an excuse.

"I know it hurts, Ebs. Only the great ones can deal with the pain," he'd say. "Can you fight through it? That's the question. A-ight? Now let's see what you got."

The workouts changed with my age and the level of commitment my sports required. The mindset was permanent, handed down from my father to me. I didn't start out wanting to deadlift the world. I was six. I just wanted to hang out with my dad. He just wanted to hang out with me. "Grab that broomstick, Nate. Let me show you the right way to bench-press."

Over the years, our dedication to working out—in the gym, on our bikes, on the squash courts and rowing machines at the Athletic Club of Columbus, even in motel rooms on vacation—never ebbed. Our commitment was always sublime and sometimes ridiculous. We did burpees at interstate rest areas.

We floated in the same chalk cloud. He had an ability to make hard work fun. I struggle to define exactly how he did this. It was such a delicate job. What twelve-year-old relishes lifting weights until he thinks his arms are going to fall off? It took a special person to make me feel that way. I like this quote, from the philosopher Simone Weil: "Attention is the rarest and purest form of generosity." That was Jeff Ebner.

. . .

AFTER MY FATHER AND my mother split, amicably, when I was an infant, my mother moved to Mason, Ohio, a suburb north of Cincinnati and an hour from our house in Springfield. Legally, my dad had me every other weekend; actually, he visited all week. After working all day at the junkyard, he'd drive an hour to Mason. We'd go to dinner, he'd help me with homework. He even joined the local YMCA so we could work out together. Then he'd drive an hour home. Nearly every weeknight.

Maybe other fathers do this. I don't know. Mine did.

Weekends we spent completely together. When you had his attention, nothing else mattered to him. He was all in. My stepmother, Amy, said she felt "protected" around my dad. When they were dating, he'd call Tuesday to arrange a date Friday night. He sent her cards constantly. Signed them "Junkman." Of course, being my dad, he couldn't resist adding the occasional Jeff Ebner slice of advice. "Adjust. Modify. Adapt." was written in one card. It became Amy's favorite.

My dad loved to talk, a skill I didn't inherit. (He didn't ration the blunt opinions, either, another trait we don't share.) He was also a good listener, always in the moment if a friend or family member needed to talk. He was empathetic with everyone but me. With me it was, "I know, Nate, but you've got to fight through it." He'd never allow for the possibility that today was a bad day, so let's just knock off early and get after it tomorrow. He wouldn't allow me to give in to myself that way. No bitching allowed.

I'm still that way. Empathy is not one of my strengths. Unless it's tragic, I'm usually not moved. You have a cold? The weather is awful? Suck it up. We all have stuffy noses, we can't change the snowstorm. If you want me to help you solve a problem, say so. Otherwise, I'll just ask you if you're bitching and tell you to stop. It's fine.

Being a good parent is more about feel than rules. My dad's goodness felt like the York barbell and the resistance of the rowing machine. Like a verbal palm on the small of my back. Like the calm I felt whenever I knew my dad was driving to Mason, Ohio, just to see me.

He was in the moment, every moment. He could be hard on me, but never on my spirit.

Jeff Ebner had shaped my mindset by the time I was sixteen. There was nothing I couldn't have if I worked for it. And I would outwork everyone.

IN THE DAYS AND WEEKS after my dad died, murdered by a thief at the junkyard when I was nineteen, the weight room became my refuge, so much that my mother and stepfather urged me to ease off, fearful I would hurt myself. They didn't realize I needed the physicality. I worked out in the basement of my mother's house, using the same gnarly plates and contraptions Jeff and I had used together. I worked out because I was desperate to feel the feelings of accomplishment we shared after grinding through a workout session. "You made 'em grow today," he'd say. I wanted to hear that. At the same time, the workouts were also a way to forget about how my dad's life ended. It was a cruel contradiction only I understood.

At that point, as I prepared to walk on at Ohio State, there wasn't a physical pain I wasn't willing to endure. At least I was feeling something. I was numb to everything else.

Two decades have passed and nothing has changed. Moments of pain and sweat make me feel closest to my dad. When I'm feeling sorry for myself or my knees hurt, I reflect on my roots. It's in my coding to go hard. I do it to honor my dad.

FOUR

On Sundays, We'd Chase Robbers

My great-great-grandfather Nathan Ebner came to America from Austria in 1883, when he was twenty-seven years old. He didn't speak English. He didn't know where he would go once he got here, or what he would do. In the final minutes of his boat passage across the Atlantic, Nathan stood at the bow of a steamship packed with would-be Americans. The ship neared Castle Garden, the immigration station at the southern tip of Manhattan.

"Where are you going?" Nathan asked the man standing next to him. They'd developed a friendship during the journey, bonded by religion. Both were Orthodox Jews.

"I'm going to Springfield, Ohio," the man answered. There was an Orthodox Jewish community in Springfield.

Nathan said, "I think I'll go to Springfield, Ohio, too."

That's how the Ebners came to America. A man leaves his homeland with just one goal, to come to this country. He doesn't speak the language, no family awaits him, he has no immediate means of supporting himself.

In Springfield, Nathan Ebner became a ragman. He picked through other people's trash, finding things he could fix and re-sell. You could think of him as one of America's original recyclers. He'd scavenge scrap metal. Copper and tin cans, mostly. Rags, too. Nathan operated out of a shack alongside the railroad. Nathan had a cart, a horse, and his ingenuity. He lived by his wits and his will, self-made, trusting the way he did things without wor-rying what other people thought.

The business worked out, and Nathan moved to a larger build-ing. By the late 1890s he had sixty employees. "Thirty men are employed in sorting, shearing, breaking, loading and unloading iron," he wrote in a Springfield newspaper early in the twentieth century. "Three baling machines work overtime getting rags and discarded clothing and linens ready for market."

In 1900, Nathan Ebner bought a piece of land at the corner of what are now North and Water Streets in downtown Spring-field. Ebner's has been there ever since.

Ebner's has evolved over the decades. My grandfather Dick Ebner ran it for years. My dad took it over in the 1980s. We don't take in scrap metal anymore, just junked cars. Running a junk-yard isn't a desk job, and cars never stop dying. Anyone doing this kind of work better be a tough guy, with a work ethic as relentless as the crusher we used to flatten junkers.

The work suited my dad. In some ways, it defined him. He could take things apart. He could put them back together, though never as good as they were, and never, ever with anyone's paid help. He wasn't about pretense, he didn't care about image. There is no caring about image at a junkyard. Who you saw was who he was. At the yard, my dad was his own boss and kept his own hours. That allowed him to play rugby, travel to tournaments on weekends, and spend lots of time with me.

He could be a violent dude. Five nine, 180, covered head to toe in hair. Dense, a damned wildebeest. He had no problem getting physical with those who tried to take what was his. Stealing was a regular occurrence at Ebner's. Lowlifes were always looking for tires, tire rims, batteries, catalytic converters (for the platinum they contained), and sound systems. Anything they could sell. Nothing pissed off my dad more than people stealing from him. He never called the cops right away. He could fix the problem himself, more quickly and efficiently. He'd make what he called a "citizen's arrest."

"You can be polite and have people continue to disrespect you," my dad said. "Or you can take matters into your own hands. We're not dealing with nice people here."

When I was a kid, I didn't see Ebner's as a violent place decorated in broken glass and dead cars. It was my personal playground. My friends and I spent summer days roaming the yard like pirates. "You wanna ride our dirt bikes first, or break stuff?" I'd ask. That was my childhood. It's hard to imagine any kid having more fun for free than I did roaming the wrecks at Ebner's.

My friends from Mason would come up for the day to smash windshields with baseball bats and car bodies with hammers. Any junk that wasn't flattened, we'd flatten.

We made steel necklaces bearing our initials and buffed them until they gleamed. We drilled holes in the steel and put the chain through each letter, like a pendant. It worked better as a concept. Each pendant weighed about ten pounds. Our necklaces were better weapons than jewelry.

We rode dirt bikes around the two-acre property, blowing tire after tire on the pieces of glass and jagged metal that were the junkyard's carpet. I'd use the loader—a gigantic, forklift-looking hunk of equipment used to scoop up crushed vehicles and transport them to a waiting semitruck—to cut highways through the yard for the bikes.

In our teens, we graduated to playing paintball. I'd use the loader to stack three or four car carcasses on top of each other, so our paintball arena would include ten-foot walls of cars to hide behind. It looked like a battle scene from a Mad Max movie.

On weekends, my dad would join us, wearing nothing but rugby shorts. He had an eight-shot pistol that had to be pumped after every shot. He'd climb a billboard just outside the yard and scream, "Come and get me!" He was outmanned and outgunned, and we pounded him without mercy until he was covered in welts.

I started working at the junkyard the summer I was fourteen. I still broke stuff, but with a purpose beyond just wanton, reckless fun. Someone would bring in a beater, I'd remove the platinum from the catalytic converter. I'd prep cars for crushing (drain the gas, pop the tires) and I'd load the crushed carcasses onto semitrucks.

The junkyard was a gnarly little world, a hundred degrees in the shade, only there wasn't any shade. Sun popping off metal, sun glinting off the broken glass. Heat making you want to lie down. And that was before noon. All spent negotiating the two acres of turf meant to hurt you. Metal and glass spiked up from the ground, aimed at your shoes.

My dad never missed work. Never. He wore what he called his "dress blues": light blue collared shirt, dark blue pants. He owned five sets. They had to be cotton, because synthetics can catch fire. They had to be dry-cleaned. Normal washing couldn't remove the grease stains or the smell of gasoline. If he was going out to eat after work, he'd exchange the dirty light blue collared shirt for a clean one. It was fine. It had a collar and buttons. In his dress blues, my dad considered himself properly attired for any occasion.

It was basically a four-man operation. My grandfather Dick worked in the "office": a ten-by-ten room just inside the entrance. Plywood, unfinished walls, a wheezing window air conditioner and a pot filled with accumulated coffee sludge. A handwritten sign: CASH ONLY. Dick answered the phone when the towing companies called.

There was nothing elegant about Ebner's. These days, junkyards are computerized and more efficient. Ebner's was as advanced as the gym behind our garage. My dad's "locker room" was a plywood-and-two-by-four loft he built above my grandfather's space. You reached it by climbing a ladder.

Ebner's had an assortment of big dogs around the place. They were mainly for show. Reecie was a 180-pound Rottweiler with a bark that sounded like the end of days. Only, he couldn't catch a thief if the guy looked like a T-bone steak. We had other dogs, equally imposing and also relatively useless. Then the robbers started poisoning our dogs, and we stopped having them.

The two-acre lot was organized, but only if you were my dad. There was no fancy computer system into which all the vehicles, and the parts they contained, were logged. My dad used an Excel spreadsheet, with all the vehicles listed in alphabetical order. If you wanted a hubcap for your '65 Mustang, you'd take your chances on my dad knowing if we had one, or where it was.

After work, I cleaned up in an outhouse-looking shed in a far corner of the lot. The soap bar was dirtier than my hands.

There were usually two workers. My dad called us yard slaves. The "super yard slave" picked up loose steel around the yard, slashed tires before vehicles were fed to the crusher, tarred the roof, swept the floors, cut what passed for grass out front, and every few years covered the EBNER'S AUTO PARTS sign with something resembling paint. It was more like oil-based oil.

It took me a summer at least to graduate from super yard slave to yard slave. The yard slave did some of the more complex jobs: running the crusher and loader, removing catalytic converters and aluminum tire rims. The original crusher was nothing but a big, square metal plate attached to a crane. You shoved a car under the crane, released the metal plate and let gravity do its thing. Like a wrecking ball. It was fine. The loader was a Cadillac in comparison. "The luxury vehicle" my dad called it. It had a radio and a roof.

My dad, the boss, did a little of everything. He took parts off vehicles, removed windshields, and made business decisions. Jeff Ebner was the one who decided when we'd crush and load cars and when we'd crush them and keep them around, to wait for the price of steel to rise. He was elite at keeping things going, even if his methods could be crazily unconventional.

And he beat up robbers.

It was love-hate work for him. He hated petty thieves. Their work was a personal affront. "I work my tail off to make a living for my family, and you think you can just walk in here with a screwdriver and a pair of bolt cutters and take what I've worked for?"

He'd say, "Nate, these are the type of people you don't want to be. Stealing scum of the earth who take the easy way out."

He loved the justice in people getting what they deserved. It didn't matter if he caused them a little pain. Running down low-lifes was just a more basic, less sporting way for him to get his smashes in.

I was ten when I got my first exposure to Jeff Ebner's badass ways. My dad had picked me up from my mom's house in Mason. I'd fallen asleep on the way to Springfield. I woke up to see police car lights flashing and my dad's hands around the necks of two perps. "They picked the wrong day to rob my yard," he explained.

When I was twelve, our bikes were stolen one Saturday in front of a Dollar Store as we shopped inside.

"That sucks," I said.

"Motherfuckers stole our bikes," Dad said.

We walked home from there, then my dad drove around Springfield all day, confident he'd make a citizen's arrest. The Springfield cops gave him a lot of latitude. They had better things to do than track down bicycle thieves.

A few hours later, my dad found the bikes and the thief, in front of someone's house. My dad knocked on the door, told the person who answered to call 911, then threw the thief off my bike. The kid ran, my dad chased him, caught him, and rode him like a sled down the sidewalk. The kid tried to press charges for the beatdown. He wasn't successful.

Springfield, Ohio, population 59,000, will never be listed among America's Best Small Cities. It looks like a lot of older places in the Rust Belt Midwest, with its loss of good-paying, blue-collar jobs, its high crime rate, its shuttered businesses (except the check-cashing places) with their windows busted out. If Springfield ever had a golden era, it came and went a long time ago. Cracked sidewalks, elderly Victorian homes falling apart. Graffiti.

To make a point, my dad would drive me around town. We'd pass through the decay. "Take a look at this," he'd say. "This isn't a place you want to be."

I wasn't immune to the violence. I was pistol-whipped when I was eleven, right outside the yard. I was moving a four-wheeler into the impound lot, when a guy walked up and smacked me in the head with his pistol. He'd been looking for his missing four-wheeler, not knowing the city had taken it from him. I happened to be the one riding it, into the lot. The pistol caught my helmet and then my eyebrow. Five stitches later, I was back in the junkyard, an eleven-year-old a little wiser in the ways of bad people.

By the time I was sixteen, chasing robbers was a Sunday ritual. Maybe you think you had a dad with whom you shared everything. You probably didn't share this.

My dad had stock ways to catch a thief. The point was always to make the robber run. That way, my dad could say he confronted the guy, the guy ran, he chased him and eventually caught him.

At that point, the robber might choose to fight, usually wielding the same tool he'd used to steal something from one of our junkers. Big mistake, bigger license for my dad to get in major smashes. If the robber chose to fight, my dad could argue he was simply defending himself. His thinking was, *I'm going to give you a head start. Because I am in good shape, I'm going to catch you, and once I do, you'll be exhausted and I will make it so you'll never come back to my junkyard again.*

He always called the police. After the fact. He couldn't afford to wait for the cops to show up while the thief was running away. As I got older, I became Jeff Ebner's coconspirator.

The thieving mostly happened on Sundays, when the yard was closed. We'd dress out in our rugby cleats and mouthpieces. We'd stretch for the battle to come. We'd hide. We'd wait.

My dad purposely made it easy for thieves to escape the yard. He'd leave a hole in the corrugated metal fence that surrounded the yard, an exit that perps always took advantage of. One, because it was the only way out and, two, because petty thieves aren't the brightest people.

My job was to confront the robber in the yard, politely. "Can I help you?" I'd say. "We're closed today."

Usually, the lowlife would take off at a dead run, toward the hole in the fence. I'd chase him, he'd run straight out the hole and into my dad, who would drop the dude like he was five pounds of flour. Occasionally, they'd have a conversation.

"What are you doing?" Dad would ask the robber.

"Nothing," the robber would say. Often enough, he'd be wearing an oversized jacket, pockets bulging.

"You're stealing from my junkyard."

"No, I'm not."

At that point, Jeff Ebner would grab the perp and shake him until parts started falling like hail from his jacket pockets. "I'll remember your face," my dad would say, letting them ponder, "Is stealing from us worth a broken nose?"

In the rare instance a robber would get away from my dad, it was temporary. The minute it became a cardiovascular event, the thief stood no chance. Attempted robberies happened all the time, and almost always Dad would offer a citizen's arrest that necessitated physical harm. He'd bring all the negative energy he could to the fight. Bad day, bad week, routine things that pissed him off. Then he'd beat the shit out of the guy.

It was very rare to see the same hombre twice. My dad's reputation for busting up robbers was well established. Occasionally, the robbers would take him to court, hoping to charge him with assault and battery or excessive use of force. My dad's standard defense was, "Aw, fuck 'em. Let 'em sue me. I had to make a citizen's arrest. I had to defend myself. Guy was stealing from me. Guy had a screwdriver."

Working at the yard was like boot camp, if boot camp came with petty thieves. The same Ebner ethos we used in the weight room applied at the junkyard. "Cars don't crush themselves, Eb," Dad would say to me.

The circumstances didn't matter to him. Hot weather? "Drink water."

Tired? "Then go to bed early tonight."

Bored/bugged/don't feel like working? "Who feels like working in a junkyard? Don't whine. It's not productive."

My dad wasn't a tyrant. "I get it, man. It's hot out here. You're tarring that roof, and it's gotta be a hundred degrees up there.

Most people couldn't do what you're doing. They'd give in to themselves.

"You can't control the heat and the aches and pains of a physically demanding job. You can control your attitude and your fortitude. Just do the work. Finish what you start, because I've got my own work to do." Those were the days that made me stronger. I didn't want a future that involved repurposing junk.

There was nothing deep about the lessons learned at Ebner's Auto Parts. Do your job, don't bitch, hit the robbers hard, and don't wash your hands with dirty soap if you can avoid it. Everything I've leaned on in tough times comes back to what I learned from my dad, and a lot of that teaching happened at the yard.

But not all of it.

There's Jeff Ebner, bombing down I-95 wearing a pair of clunky, old-man headphones and watching a movie on the DVD player mounted to the dash. He had a lot of quirks. He'd have been an unusual guy even without them. His collection of eccentricities only made him more unique. My dad had a lot of character. Occasionally, he was one.

He'd beat up robbers at the junkyard, then go home and read *The Bridges of Madison County*.

Nothing mattered more to him than his physical condition, and the discipline it took to maintain. He adhered to this logic, expressed by Socrates:

"No man has the right to be an amateur in the matter of physical training. It is a shame for a man to grow old without seeing the beauty and strength of which his body is capable."

Yet he'd order dessert first at a restaurant. Sometimes more than one dessert, his thinking being he loved dessert and never wanted to be so full he couldn't enjoy it. "If I don't have room at the end, at least I had all my favorites," was his explanation.

He and his buddy Mike Garcia once consumed eight appetizers in one sitting at Bonefish Grill.

Naturally, our relationship was influenced by my dad's personality.

I was fifteen when my dad and I and three of my high school rugby teammates went to Savannah, Georgia, for a tournament during spring break. I was driving. Legally, because a licensed driver was with me. Jeff Ebner was riding shotgun, reading the newspaper. My friends were in the back.

The discussion took an interesting turn when one of my friends asked, "Do you think you could take your dad" in a fight?

"This old man next to me?" I said. "I can take him."

My buddies found this interesting. They asked me to elaborate. My dad continued to read.

"He's an old man and I'm a young bull. I'm too fast for him," I said. This went on for a few minutes. I was feeling pretty chesty.

"Pull over," Jeff Ebner said.

We're on the interstate, doing about seventy miles an hour. "What?"

"Pull the car over."

I complied. "Get out," said my father. "Square up."

For some reason, I said, "Let's do this." And we did.

My dad put both hands over his head and started waving

them. Weirdly distracting. Then he hit me with a double-leg takedown. I was on my back in five seconds. Then he leveled his fist an inch from my face. Like a samurai bringing his sword to an opponent's throat.

We got up, dusted ourselves off, got in the car, and drove to Savannah without further discussion.

The message? Beyond reaffirming who was boss?

Walk the talk. If you're going to make a statement, be ready to back it up or keep your mouth shut.

My dad was a violent dude, without being overly aggressive. Most people threaten mayhem. My dad lived it. He wouldn't walk away, especially not out of fear.

He and I were nearly best friends by then. By the time I graduated from high school, the typical father-son relationship had been ousted. We saw each other more as peers. That didn't mean he stopped teaching lessons. Once a father . . .

After we played in Savannah, we drove to Clearwater, Florida, to visit relatives. My friends and I stayed in a hotel room on the beach. My dad was next door.

We decided to do the town one night. My dad had let us drink beers in an establishment in Savannah, mainly because he wanted to observe how responsibly I might or might not act. I must have passed his test, because there we were a few nights later, repeating the scene in Clearwater.

My friends and I were out quite a while. We had a good time. Until Jeff Ebner let himself into our room at eight the next morning.

"Rise and shine!" His voice smashed into my brainpan like a brick through glass. "I don't care if you guys go out at night," he said, "but you are going to get up the next morning and work out."

As a member of the Scioto Valley Rugby Club, he'd had considerable experience burning both ends of the candle. He'd party hard Saturday and play hard Sunday. It was a point of pride. "What kind of a player are you on Sundays?" was a frequent question among the guys in the Scioto Valley Rugby Club.

We went to the beach and ran for two hours. I was the only one among us who didn't throw up. "You gotta pay to play," my dad said. It was a simple and totally unpleasant reminder that actions have consequences and success doesn't happen without discipline and responsibility.

To this day, I am not a big drinker.

One more thing: Sometime after my friends and I returned from our night of fun, one of the guys punched a hole in the hotel room wall. The next morning, my dad sat patiently in our room, examining the hole, and wondering how much of his money it was going to take to repair.

"Who did this?"

"Tommy!" we agreed, in unison.

My dad waited for Tommy Fetters to get out of the shower. When he did, wearing a towel the size of a floor mat, my dad grabbed him by the throat and slammed him on the bed. Tommy's towel flew off. He had 180 pounds of pissed off on top of his naked self.

"Don't ruin this trip for everyone else," my dad said. "And you're going to pay for that hole."

My dad wasn't screaming. He sounded like a librarian reminding a patron that his book was overdue. Hours later, Tommy was still stressing. "Mr. Ebs hates me," he said. "I fucked up, man. I fucked up."

"It's all good, man," I said. "He slammed you and said his stuff. It's behind him now. Just don't be punching any more walls."

FIVE

It's Fine

The junkyard defined my dad, but only during the hours he was there. He didn't live to work. Before he came home to Springfield to run Ebner's, he'd graduated from the University of Minnesota and started a job with Electronic Data Systems in Dallas, the firm owned by H. Ross Perot. It wasn't as if running the yard challenged his brain.

But he did take his personality to Ebner's. It served him perfectly. I don't know if it's in the Ebner genes to be frugal, practical, and stubbornly independent. Great-Great-Grandpa Nathan thrived that way. The junk business depends on an ability to adapt to the junk you're faced with, literally and otherwise. I mean, it's called junk for a reason.

Above everything—and another trait that worked beautifully

at Ebner's—was Jeff Ebner's disdain for the superficial. He was utterly lacking in bullshit. He didn't care what something looked like—he didn't often care what *he* looked like—only that it could do the job.

Case in point: My dad considered himself an artist. Well, at least he believed he had artistic ability. As proof, he'd point proudly to the oil paintings on a few walls at the house. "I did those," he'd say. What he didn't say was, those fine oil paintings were paint-by-number specials. He signed them "Kingstroke."

Worrying about what other people thought of him was not in his playbook. It was a waste of energy.

Jeff Ebner was who he was. Take him or leave him, he wasn't changing for you. He had a catchall expression that he applied liberally when confronted by someone or something that ran counter to his version of how the world should work:

"It's fine."

Did I mention that this was his favorite expression? That circular dumbbell so out of plumb it doesn't even roll? "Forty-five pounds is forty-five pounds. Does it get the job done? It's fine."

The corduroy suit my dad wore, the only suit he owned? "What do I need fancy suits for?"

The duct tape, plastered on everything in the weight room, was classic It's Fine. If artfully applying duct tape made you a seamstress, my dad would be Betsy Ross.

"You think I'm an anachronism and an iconoclast? I don't even know what that means. You say I'm a little strange? So sue me. It's fine."

The jobs we did, and how we did them, were exempt from It's Fine thinking. They were important. The work could never be just fine, either at the junkyard or in the gym. Cars had to be crushed properly if we were going to stack them on a semitruck. But the machinery used in the process? Does it work? Does it get the job done? It's Fine.

I love steak. I don't love the fat on steak. Whenever my dad and I ate steak, I'd trim off the fat. This offended Jeff's sensibilities.

"What are you doing?" he wanted to know. "There's nothing wrong with fat. You're dissecting that thing."

"I don't like fat."

He'd grab the fat in his hand and move it to his plate. "It's fine," he'd say.

Taking apart our ten-ton loader required us to work beneath the beastly machine. Normally, this is a job that requires heavy-duty hydraulic jacks. My dad used stacks of wood. Honestly. Wood-for-hydraulics. It was the one time I refused to do the work. I wasn't going to sit under a ten-ton loader supported by a bunch of wood. My dad fixed the loader himself.

Was the loader nice? Of course not. It was a piece of junk, among all the junk. Did it work? Yes, it did. It was fine.

It's Fine had a bigger meaning than making do with substandard things, or paying no mind to the opinions of others. It was my dad's way of ignoring stress over things he considered meaningless. He didn't understand people who bitched about things they had to do, or had done already. They couldn't change anything, so why try?

He didn't waste a worry about dressing and undressing in public. His trunk doubled as his closet. I had friends whose lasting impressions of my dad were made the first time they'd met him, before a rugby practice, shaking his hand when he was nude. "If they wanna look, they can look," he said. He could have changed into his rugby stuff at the junkyard, then driven to practice. Why he didn't, I honestly don't know.

He wasn't an exhibitionist. He just didn't believe it mattered.

"It only counts when you're naked," he explained. To him, that meant not sweating how he appeared to the rest of the world. It was superficial bullshit, he reasoned. When you are naked having sex, you're entirely exposed. Why bother hiding yourself the rest of the time?

On my dad's first date with his second wife, Amy, he arrived at the appointed hour, opened the trunk of his car, and changed his clothes in her driveway. Amy's sixteen-year-old daughter Beth watched with interest from inside the house. "That's the hairiest man I've ever seen," she said.

"What have I gotten myself into?" was Amy's take. For the first time, she'd been exposed—pun intended—to Jeff Ebner's authenticity. If you had a problem with a guy changing clothes in your driveway, that was on you.

This is where I should say that I took from It's Fine only what I thought were its positive elements. Superficial stuff doesn't interest me, either. What people who don't know me say or think of me has never made a dent. Your opinion of how I play football has never stopped me from making a tackle. Some writer's take on my chances of making the 2016 Olympic team didn't keep me from making it.

Though I'll admit among the greatest satisfactions of my life was beating the Los Angeles Rams in the Super Bowl in 2019, when we'd heard for most of the season how washed-up the New England Patriots were.

My ability to tunnel-focus is a by-product of It's Fine. I can block out everything that doesn't apply to what I'm trying to do. Jeff Ebner's ability to strip situations bare (sometimes literally) taught me to embrace what mattered and ignore what didn't. My focus is narrow and intense. When I want something, nothing else matters.

Unlike my dad, I don't make a habit of getting dressed in public. His so-what bluntness could be off-putting to people who didn't know him. Generally, I don't offer my opinions unless I'm asked. If I don't know what I'm talking about, I won't say much. That, too, is fine.

OUR LIVES OCCURRED IN a perpetual state of Fineness. My dad never bought a new car, reasoning he could fix an older one. He preferred Mercedes. He'd buy them on the cheap at auctions.

If he could do something himself, he did. He fixed things, he built things, he never paid anyone for any of it. When we moved from the house on the busy two-lane of High Street in Spring-field to a quiet suburb, my dad decided he wanted a deck off the back of the house. When he discovered he needed a building permit, he came up with what he'd have termed a Fuck It plan.

(Fuck It and its close relative, Fuck 'Em, were descendants of the It's Fine family tree, and also favorites of Jeff Ebner's. They captured neatly a crucial aspect of his personality when it came to doing things conventionally, or behaving to suit polite society. "Maybe you shouldn't wear dress blues to a nice restaurant, Dad." "Fuck 'em," he'd say. Or maybe, "Fuck it." They were interchangeable.)

The way I understood it, if the addition were not connected to the house, he didn't need a building permit. He could avoid needing official approval, or paying for it. Jeff Ebner read up on how to build a deck, got the supplies, and made me build the deck about an inch off the back wall of the house. It's still there, more than a decade later, floating happily in its own little Fuck 'Em space, half an inch removed from the rest of the house.

When I was little, my dad owned an aging Mercedes convertible, with a hardtop that could be installed when the weather changed. The problem was, the top weighed 120 pounds, and Jeff had no one to help him install it. Most people faced with that predicament would probably drive to the dealer and pay to have the top installed.

My dad used a pulley system in his garage. He attached a rope to a garage roof beam, looped it around the hardtop, and pulled.

"Jeff, what are you doing?" Amy asked.

What does it look like I'm doing?

"Nothing, Ames. It's fine."

It's Fine could also be rooted in my dad's frugality. He always packed the washer to the max. We had a dryer, too, but he didn't use it. He hung his clothes on a line in the basement. They were stiff as two-by-fours.

It's Fine could be rooted in my dad's blissful lack of self-consciousness. Jeff Ebner wore a Casio wristwatch with five alarms on it. Once a restaurant hostess seated us, he'd set one alarm for five minutes. If it went off and we hadn't been waited on, we would leave. No exceptions.

It's Fine wasn't simply an expression. It was a filter for everything Jeff considered superfluous and nonsensical. It explained a big chunk of who he was. Purposeful, in an eccentric sort of way. If you didn't like that about him, well, fuck it. Sue him. It's fine.

SIX

Kegs on Weekends

Rugby wasn't the first connective tissue between my dad and me, only the most enduring. I played baseball as a little kid. My dad hated baseball. He'd come to all my games, but he'd spend most of his time in the bleachers, reading a newspaper. Except when I messed up. Then he'd boo me.

I played peewee football, too. My dad never missed so much as a practice, even though he had to drive from Springfield to Mason to get there. Coaches and parents nicknamed him "On Time."

I was a good football player. Once, when my team played in a tournament at Paul Brown Stadium in Cincinnati, we walked through the parking lot past a minivan bearing this sign:

BEAT COMETS. KILL NO. 32.

I was number 32.

I stopped playing kids' football when I started playing rugby. No sport held me the way rugby did. It was my dad's passion, and it became mine. The time we spent playing together, him watching me play, even the drives to and from tournaments and practice—maybe especially those drives—were among the best of our lives.

In his Scioto Valley Rugby Club Hall of Fame speech, Jeff called me his "legacy." Steve Finkel once said my father "cared in his heart about rugby." I couldn't run from that, even if I wanted to.

Eventually, I would stop sharing my dad's approach to the game. He played for the physicality of it. There was no hit he wouldn't give or take. Red Hot was the answer to any rugby problem.

I took to the beauty of the game. Its flow. The choreography of a well-thrown pass, the integrity of a clean line, and the teamwork rugby required. The constant search for space and when it all came together, a well-executed try. That's what hooked me.

Rugby has everything. It's the ultimate trial of an athlete, testing endurance and strength. You can be big and strong in football, but you don't have to run very long. In soccer, you have to run but you don't have to be strong and you can't hit anybody.

What if, say, Bo Jackson had wanted to play rugby? Two-sport star, amazing strength and speed. Could he have passed the ball *and* kicked it? How would he have felt about having to tackle people all day, while constantly running what amounted to forty-yard dashes?

Elite Sevens players are the best-conditioned athletes in the world. If you're big and play football, they're going to put you on the offensive line. All you'll do is block people. Don't jump offside, don't hold, just control this monster in front of you. If you're lucky, you'll play more than a few years and retire without needing to pop Advils like breath mints. In rugby, you might be better at one part of the game than others, but you have to do the others anyway. Everybody does everything.

If one teammate doesn't do his job, the whole team suffers for it. There is room for individual stars, but they have to play within the demands of the team.

I loved working out. Playing rugby—Sevens or Fifteens—was an extended workout. There is no cardio workout that can match Sevens rugby. Two seven-minute halves, no stopping, nothing but running and tackling, getting up and running some more. Soccer players don't tackle. Football players wear armor. Rugby players wear mouthpieces. As my dad put it, the only pads in rugby are the ones you build in the weight room.

Rugby has no time-outs. Rugby doesn't stop. Players think on their feet. Rugby, especially Sevens, has the speed and flow of basketball without the timeouts.

It wasn't just the game itself, though. Rugby produces a unique band of brothers. It doesn't matter what level you play the game.

The camaraderie, the shared experiences, the parties, the pain. It's a special subculture. You can walk into any rugby club in the world, tell them you play the game, and instantly have fifty new friends. It's an informal family, with all of a family's morals, values, and spirit.

As I progressed up the ranks, the cultural opportunities rugby presented made me love the game even more. Americans who see the world become more grateful for what they have at home. Travel with the Junior World Cup team never stopped giving me a fresh perspective on how lucky I am to live in the States. That rugby brotherhood gets tighter on the road, too. It's one thing to share a practice facility with your peers, the way NFL teams do. It's another to spend weeks at a time on the road, in places where the language and customs are nothing like ours.

After that first B-side game when I was thirteen, I played Sevens all summer for Scioto Valley. Tuesdays and Thursdays after working at the junkyard, we'd load the pickup with our rugby kits, the disgusting plastic water jug, and Magnum, the dog, and head for practice in Columbus, forty-five minutes away. On weekends, we played in tournaments all over the Midwest.

As I became immersed in the world of the Scioto Valley Rugby Club, I saw why my dad loved the game so much. Even at the club level—maybe especially at that level— rugby is a straight-up, no-excuses game. Hit and be hit, then share laughs afterward. No grudges, no egos. Humility plays well in rugby, because everyone involved understands the pain of constant running and tackling. Egos are benched because no player is more important than the next.

Our weekend travels consolidated the brotherhood. Qualifying for the club nationals required accumulating points by playing in weekend tournaments and winning them. We'd be somewhere every weekend all spring and summer: Cleveland, Ohio; Chicago, Illinois; Louisville, Kentucky; Elkhart, Indiana. We'd meet up at our practice field after work on Friday and caravan to the tournament.

Saturday mornings, we'd find some shade near the tournament fields and unfurl our traveling living room: lawn chairs, canopies, first-aid kits, and massive plastic coolers containing water for while we played and beer for when we were done. From that perspective, club rugby tournaments were no different from any soccer or softball event that stretched through a weekend. Except that after five matches of Sevens in one day, you can barely curl a beer from your hand to your mouth.

In the summer heat, the beers went down easily, their effects quickly felt. To some guys, the matches were the penance paid for the drinking afterward. They'd rate our opponents on how good their after-parties were, and on the attractiveness of their clubhouses. Grown men, barbarians at the gate, barnstorming on weekends, unsupervised and free to act like boys. Does anything sound more perfect when you're a thirty-year-old man?

I wasn't a man. I was fourteen, fifteen, sixteen when I played for Scioto Valley. The social aspect of the club remained foreign to me. I didn't want to drink and I was born serious. A light heart was not something I got from my dad. I was there to learn rugby, not drink beer.

Rugby wasn't a weekend pleasure to me, or a way to relive my high school glory days. It was serious business. Besides, I was too young to drink. Which made me the perfect chauffeur for my dad. As soon as I got my driver's license, I became his designated driver.

By then, Jeff Ebner was too old to play regularly for the Scioto Sevens. He'd go on weekends to watch me and hang out with his friends still playing. That said, he always packed his kit and his Red Hot in the trunk, in case a team needed players.

More than once after a tournament, I'd be driving my dad's ancient Mercedes 550 SL, while Jeff Ebner and Steve Finkel loitered in the back seat, knocking back beers and watching adult videos on the portable DVD player. Finkel was my dad's closest friend and running buddy. They shared a love for rugby and women, not always in that order.

THINGS CHANGED FOR THE Valley boys in 2006. The side from Columbus, Ohio, took a season off from the frat house vibe so familiar to club rugby. Scioto Valley was very good, good enough to qualify for nationals. The partying didn't stop completely. This was, after all, club rugby. It just ebbed.

This was OK by me. I was learning on my own to love the sport my dad loved. I didn't need his urging, which always had been the way he wanted it. "I don't ever want to leave a bad taste in your mouth," he said. My dad wanted me to love the game, but he wanted me to love everything we did, from running hills to crushing dead cars. Love the competition, enjoy the work you put in, because it's the work away from the games that allows you the joy during the games. "This game isn't fun when you're tired," he'd say.

He'd turn our drives home from games and practices into postgame highlight shows. "Great smash you put on that guy," he'd say. "Nice hustle running him down. Passing with both hands now? Great try from the corner." He wasn't grooming me for greatness. He just wanted me to enjoy what I was doing. Young kids are sponges. I was a sponge and I was around some good players. I watched my dad tackle, because he was great at it. But when it came to the nuances practiced by better players, I watched other guys.

I streamed rugby on TV. The rugby World Cup, the Tri-Nations tournament, the British Lions. Dan Carter, my favorite player, a fly half for the world's best team, the All Blacks of New Zealand. I studied. I was obsessed.

My affection for rugby grew with my ability to play it. It's not a sport learned anywhere but in the throes of doing it. The irony was, the better I got and the more interested I became, the less I looked to my dad for instruction.

He was the consummate club player. What my dad lacked in skills and nuance, he made up for in fearlessness and physicality. I enjoyed that part of it, too, but there came a time when I needed to graduate. The club game lacked the little things I'd need to play internationally. The checkers-to-chess analogy is overworked, but apt in this case.

I already had good physical skills. At twelve, I could pass with both hands better than my dad. When I was fourteen, I ran down and tackled Ron Bowers, a Scioto Valley teammate and my future coach at Ohio State. (My dad, naturally, couldn't resist busting Ron for that. "Looks like your time is up, Bow," he said.)

But I was far from a finished product. I needed to learn the insider's game. I needed to see things on the pitch the average fan didn't see. Skills, without the knowledge to use them properly, are just skills. The subtleties, not the smashes, would get me to an elite level.

I began to watch Elliot Pollard, a Scioto Valley teammate who'd grown up with the game in South Africa. Elliot was thirteen years my senior. We shared similar rugby frustrations, though his were on a higher level than mine. Elliot felt about Scioto Valley the way I would about high school and college rugby. The lack of competition frustrated him.

Pollard played rugby all through grade school, until he broke his collarbone. He began playing touch rugby on the beach. He said he learned more on the beach than from any coach he ever had.

The better club teams passed him by. Beach rugby didn't attract much attention. Frustrated at being passed over, Elliot sought opportunities overseas. He read something in the local paper about a club league in San Diego seeking players. He took a flyer.

When he got to San Diego, Pollard didn't find a finely groomed pitch filled with experienced players. "Where's the stadium?" he asked. A guy pointed to what Pollard called a "cow pasture." Pollard wanted to know where he might change. He was directed to a porta-potty. Rugby in the US.

The first few years I played Sevens with Scioto Valley, I played a lot of junk time in lesser tournaments. I was learning a lot, from Finkel and Pollard, who, as a center, played next to me. I was the fly half, the Sevens version of a basketball point guard. I learned some of high-level rugby's essential dancing. When to pass, when to run. How to draw a defense to me. I learned that space was rugby's holy grail: the need for it, how to create it for myself and my mates, how to recognize space and how to best exploit it.

Pollard inspired me. *So this is what the game can look like.* He was a visual player. He understood what was happening around him. He saw the peripheries. Watching him made me aware of my own possibilities. There was more to rugby than catching, running, and smashing. It could be both brutish and beautiful. I knew the brute side already. I played alongside my father. Space awareness, how to find space, how to create space for a teammate, with or without the ball, became my obsession. I was playing fly half by then. Finding space for myself and others was my job.

And truthfully, space awareness for me was a form of self-defense. My growth spurt came late. When I was playing in men's games at age fifteen, I was not physically dominant or imposing my will on anyone. Seeing space and running to it might have saved me from getting clobbered a few times.

The 2006 club qualified for the nationals in Ferndale, Washington. We were seeded sixteenth of sixteen. We knew we were better than that. Ferndale would be the high-water mark of my club rugby days. I appreciated Scioto Valley for what it taught me: tackling, running, scoring tries. The close-knit, in-the-moment joy taken from weekend roadies and the parties before and after. I understood why some guys on that team would call those times the best of their lives.

Only now, I needed to graduate. Ferndale would be both a satisfying end and a glorious beginning.

SEVEN

Hitting My Rugby Stride, and Walking Away

When you're seventeen and in love, you don't think past the next minute. In barely three years, I would go from playing in my first match with the Scioto men to becoming a member of our national rugby team and playing in the Junior World Cup.

My swift move up the ranks said two things about the state of rugby in America near the turn of the twenty-first century: (1) I was good at the game and (2) America's progress didn't mimic mine. In Britain or South Africa, it's rare to see even the best youth rugby players go from playing their first club match to playing for their country in the Junior World Cup in just three years.

I would be twenty years old and a sophomore at Ohio State

before it occurred to me that playing the game I loved would be a professional dead end in the United States. Until then, I was obsessed with learning to be the player I wanted to be.

Before Ferndale, there was Dubai, and before Dubai, there was Arizona. My rugby career was moving fast. In two years, 2005 and 2006, this was my résumé:

FALL 2005: Developmental camp with the US Under-19 team.

SPRING 2006: Member of the US Junior World Cup team in Dubai.

SUMMER 2006: Played for Scioto Valley Rugby Club in the men's national club Sevens championships.

FALL 2006: Attended camp with the national Men's Sevens team. Played for the Under-19s nationally and internationally.

Looking back, I have a hard time keeping the calendar straight. I've never learned so much, so fast. It started with a conversation Steve Finkel had with a man named Wilbert "Salty" Thompson, in the fall of 2005, nearly a year before Ferndale.

"I have a player you need to look at," Finkel said.

Thompson was the coach of the US Under-19 team. He ended up inviting me to the Under-19 developmental camp. That experience ignited my national rugby career. The exposure was the proverbial foot in the door. I went to that camp as an eager sixteen-year-old, hoping just to make an impression on Thompson so he'd consider me for future camps. I ended up making our Junior World Cup team that played in Dubai in Spring 2006.

Salty brought out the best in me. We had a lot in common, not least a deep and stubborn striver's mentality.

Salty Thompson grew up in a fishing village in Northern Ireland during the Troubles. A rugby teammate nicknamed him Salty Dog, which became Salty. Which fit his temperament. "I had a bit of an edge," he recalled. Salty played scrum half. Occasionally, he punched opponents during games. He called himself "a terrier."

As an undergraduate at Loughborough University in London, Salty ran track to improve his rugby speed and stamina. As he explained, "Playing rugby is like running four hundred or eight hundred meters. Except it's continuous and there's contact. Both sports require you to push through the discomfort. Mental toughness, smile about the pain. It's a mindset."

Loughborough is well-known for producing Olympic athletes, including the legendary middle-distance runner Sebastian Coe, who won Olympic gold in 1980 and 1984. While at Loughborough, Salty served as Coe's "rabbit" in the eight hundred meters in university competitions and was a member of the school's 4-by-400 relay team, along with Coe.

Thompson the terrier relished finding his physical limits. I could relate to that. "There is a certain weird comfort when you get to three hundred meters in a four-hundred-meter race," he explained. Experienced rugby players know the feeling. We call reaching absolute exhaustion the Dark Place. Salty had no issues testing himself that way. That made him a good coach for me.

He left England in 1980 to pursue his master's in secondary education at Arizona State. He met and married his wife, then they returned to England, where he taught at Ratcliffe College, a high school with 250 male students and eight rugby teams. He taught at Ratcliffe for four years and resurrected his rugby career before returning to Arizona in 1986.

In 2003, USA Rugby appointed him coach of the Under-19 national team. I met him for the first time at that 2005 developmental camp.

I was a reserve on the Under-19 side that went to Dubai for the Junior World Cup. I wasn't just the youngest player on our team. I was the youngest player, period. We were playing against teams whose players were under contract, from countries where rugby really mattered. I was seventeen, trying to figure it out on the fly.

I did a lot of watching and listening. Most of what happens in high-level rugby—the kind played at the World Cup and in the World Series—involves skill and strategy not seen at the surface level.

In Dubai an assistant US coach named Michael Engelbrecht made a point that stuck with me:

"Think how much time you spend on a rugby pitch playing a Fifteens match [eighty minutes]. Now, think how much time the ball is actually in your hands. [Two minutes, tops.] All the work you do is off the ball. The stuff to set you up to score is done before you have the ball. We don't run down the field, stiff-arming everyone."

Rugby flows from side to side. East to west, with the intention of going north and south. You pass the ball laterally and backward to move it forward. Everything we do is about changing angles and setting up defenders so we can break through the line and go north and south. That's done with precise passing and cutting, to open up running space or to get defenders out of position. Think of a football wide receiver running a route against zone coverage and finding a hole in the zone. The point is to find and create space for yourself or your teammates.

The best players make it a downhill game. The ball flows smoothly from player to player across the field while steadily inching forward, until you find a crack in the defense. Then you hit the crack like it's the only escape from a burning building.

I understood all this stuff, in theory. I'd watched a lot of international competition on the internet and respected how Elliot Pollard played the game at Scioto Valley. I knew what to do. I was learning how to do it. But I had to adjust to the speed of the game. The players weren't as big as the competition I saw with Scioto Valley. They were much faster. Everybody could pass with both hands, everybody understood angles and leverage and how to make space. This was rugby the way I envisioned it. Brutal and lovely, a slam dance ballet. It was like going from the Soap Box Derby to Formula 1. Everything was cleaner, tighter, and faster. Everyone was a good player.

I couldn't do things the way I did them at the club level. I couldn't just catch and run. I played fullback in Dubai. Fullbacks freelance more on offense than other players. They play with some spontaneity, but where they come into the line on attack can be critical for a team's ability to score.

On defense, the fullback plays the deep middle, not unlike a safety in football. He's the last line of defense. To play fullback, you need speed, the ability to anticipate where the ball is going, and the courage to tackle well. I had the speed, and I was learning when to use it. The more I played, the better I got at anticipating the action. You simply can't miss tackles as a fullback. That's how big plays happen. For me, the son of Jeff Ebner and a veteran of club rugby smashes, tackling was never a problem.

We got to Dubai a week ahead of time, then spent the next three weeks competing. This was Fifteens, not Sevens. Eighty-minute games, not fourteen minutes. Not as taxing on your lungs, more taxing on your body. We didn't play several games in a day. We played one game every five days.

I got back home and reunited with the Scioto Valley Sevens. The international games had made me a better player. It was my first full season with the club, and it ended in Ferndale, Washington, at the national club Sevens championships.

The weekend warrior stereotype didn't apply often at nationals. This was the highest level of club rugby in the country.

Anybody could understand Steve Finkel's explanation for how he wanted us to play offense at Ferndale: "Keep it away from the shit." Scioto's players knew exactly what he meant. Finkel's idea was to create space on offense by stretching and wearing out the defense. Avoid contact. As soon as you're in trouble, make a pass. Moving backward was OK, if it meant keeping the ball. Possession was everything. It required us to work very hard off the ball. Lots of running, even by Sevens standards. The offensive plan required everyone to be on script. That was revolutionary at the club level.

Scioto had been playing offense that way all summer. At best, it was unorthodox. At worst, it was at odds with the entire club rugby culture. You mean, when we're on attack, we're not going to attack? You want us to play . . . *keep-away*?

Essentially, yeah.

It worked. We frustrated and wore down defenses. In any sport, exhaustion impairs decision making. Defenses tired, then one of two things would happen: Elliot Pollard and I gashed them up the middle, or our teammate Kevin Mongold "skinned" them on the outside, meaning he got around the defense on the edge of the pitch. It all depended on how defenses played us.

Seeded sixteenth in the championships out of sixteen, we finished sixth. It was a big achievement for a bunch of guys from Ohio who liked to smash people and drink beer. For me, it was bigger than that. That year, Steve Finkel revealed for me the magic of the sport. He validated my experiences in Dubai. There was another, higher level of rugby, and it was beautiful.

I was learning how to break down a defense. I was beginning to think about the game at a high level. In a sport with no time-outs or time for a coach to coach from the sideline, using the mind matters.

Finkel explained to me the idea of creating an overlap. Think about a two-on-one fast break in basketball. The goal is to have more players on attack than the other team can defend. You create an overlap by making a pass, then looping behind the receiver before the defense can slide out to mark the extra man you just created.

It was an aha moment for me. I could use my body to make room for myself and others. I could change angles and run inside lines if the defense was too quick to play us outside, or outside lines if they were staying compact. I could pass off both hands. The more I played, the more I saw what the best players were doing, and how they were doing it. I tried to make it instinctual even if my choices were wrong at times. Thinking takes time. Time is speed. I can still hear Elliot Pollard: "Maybe you should pass it in that situation, mate."

We had a good tournament. Our sixth-place finish was among the best ever for an Ohio club. I played well in my first club event outside the Midwest. I didn't know that important people in the national rugby world were there, including Al Caravelli, who was scouting prospects for the US Sevens men's team. He'd just been named head coach. Caravelli intended to completely change the perception and the roster of the team he inherited.

He asked Steve Finkel at Ferndale if Finkel had anyone on his team worth a look. As he had nearly a year earlier, to Salty

Thompson, Finkel mentioned me. "Phenomenal athlete, great feet. Seventeen years old and not afraid to tackle."

Caravelli liked the way I played. I was a homegrown talent, who actually knew the game. That was different. Those first few years coaching the national Men's Sevens, Caravelli sought athletes, not necessarily rugby players.

"I didn't look for skills," he said years later. "I could teach guys rugby. I looked for athletes. People with good feet, good speed and work ethic. Most weren't rugby players."

I was a rugby player and an athlete. I wasn't ready to be a member of Caravelli's Sevens team. I didn't have the experience. Physically, I was still growing into my body. Caravelli saw my potential, though. That fall of 2006, he persuaded Salty Thompson to let me attend the Sevens training camp at the US Military Academy.

In one year, I went from the knockaround and joyous obscurity of club rugby to training camp with our national Men's Sevens team. My head needed a better swivel.

The next two years, I played for Salty Thompson on the junior national team. In Dubai in 2006, I was just trying to keep up. I came into my own the next year, the spring of 2007, in Ireland, playing every minute of every game at fullback. In Wales in 2008, when the Under-19 team became the Under-20 squad, I was at my best. I played fullback, but also outside center, a position that demanded that I create space for my teammates playing outside of me. (Very rarely I played other positions too, as needed—I played wherever Salty Thompson needed me.)

The World Cup is the US national team's biggest international competition. We played the Canadian national team in the Freedom Cup. We played in the Pan Am Games. We played college sides and good club sides. But the best competition on the biggest stage—the matches where I knew I'd improve—was always at the World Cup.

I came home from my first two Junior World Cups to play for my high school team, an experience both surreal and frustrating. One day, I'm playing against South Africa, a team with twenty-two of its twenty-six players on pro contracts. The next day, I'm telling a kid who was the starting middle linebacker at Hilliard Davidson High School that on a rugby pitch, he can't flatten an opponent after the guy kicks the ball.

I was nineteen and in the middle of my third year of Junior World Cup play when I enrolled at Ohio State. I joined the Fifteens team there. Ron Bowers, my old Scioto Valley teammate, was the coach. I felt how Elliot Pollard felt when he played with Scioto Valley. Chess, meet checkers.

Rugby was a club sport at OSU, with everything that implied. Bowers enjoyed having me on the team. "It was easy for me to coach what was already there," Bowers recalled. "I just built on what Nate had. I wanted him to learn to read what was going on, to create on the field and make him think about the game.

"There were no time-outs. I can't send in plays. Once it starts, it's on. You need guys who know what they're doing.

"Nate understood how to break down a defense. How to

create a two-on-one overload. It's all about fourteen guys putting away that fifteenth guy. Plus, Nate had that speed. That allowed him to use all his other skills. He was fast, he could think the game, he wouldn't be denied. And he was a great tackler. Tackling separates the men from the boys."

Bowers also understood that for me, playing club ball after playing overseas was incurably aggravating. "He was better and more committed to rugby than anyone on our team. That frustrated him beyond belief."

Put it like this: I'd played rugby all over the world. When I came back to Ohio State, I couldn't even get in a good practice. We'd have a scrum, they couldn't get me the ball. I'd throw a pass right to one of my teammates, he'd drop it forward. Knock-on. The other team's ball. I got tired of saying, "Catch the ball!"

I couldn't even be sure that day to day everyone would come to practice. I was serious and seriously obsessed. My teammates might have been dedicated guys, but not to rugby. I couldn't be knocking on doors.

I knew they were trying. But the game didn't mean to them what it meant to me. In the 2011 Collegiate Rugby Championships against the University of California, I was running everywhere. I broke through the line five or six times. I'd start looking around, and there was no one on my team close enough to pass to. On defense, sometimes it felt like I was literally tackling everyone, because no one on my team would tackle. Eventually, I had no juice to create offensively.

One of my teammates, J.B. Strahler, later said, "Nate saw

[opportunities] nobody else saw. He wouldn't get mad, but he would say something if he thought you weren't taking it seriously."

Grinding my molars playing college club rugby made me start thinking about my future in the game. And realizing I probably didn't have one.

My career was headed down the typical American rugby road. I played three years for Salty Thompson on the Under-19 and Under-20 teams and had become a mainstay. I was also at a crossroads. Wales in the spring, club Sevens in the summer, fall at Ohio State. Then what?

I couldn't play for our Junior National team anymore. I was too old. I'd promised my parents I'd get my degree, so I couldn't travel and play for the men's national team at the same time.

I was watching the progress Al Caravelli was making with the Men's Sevens. It was impressive, but still nowhere near the level financially it needed to be to attract me to play professionally. I loved rugby, but there was no career in it unless I was willing to move overseas. I didn't want to do that.

I'd been at Ohio State for two years. I would be twenty years old that December 2008. I needed a plan. It would be a crazy plan by normal standards. It would be questioned by nearly everyone, patronized and snickered at and altogether dismissed. The only people who took it seriously at first were the two guys eating dinner together on a November night in 2008.

"I'm gonna walk on to the football team," I said to Jeff Ebner. "My goal is to get a shot at the NFL."

This was beyond ambitious. It was borderline ridiculous. I hadn't played football since eighth grade, and now I intended to walk on to one of the best college teams in the country. And use that experience as a springboard to the NFL.

Some would call it audacious, more called it ridiculous. To me, it was just testing every lesson Jeff Ebner had taught:

You can have anything if you're willing to sacrifice everything. Push through the pain. Push yourself. Other people play football at Ohio State. Why can't you?

I would become so committed to playing college football and getting a chance to play in the NFL that my quest didn't sound audacious to me. My quest became my obsession. Rugby was the casualty. I set aside my passion for what I saw as the more practical choice. I never thought rugby was over for me, however. First loves never really die. To my mind, I was simply putting rugby on pause while I explored another option. I left rugby, for a time. It never left me.

EIGHT

A Decision and
a Tragedy

I met my dad for dinner at the Athletic Club of Columbus on November 12, 2008.

My dad joined the Athletic Club of Columbus when I was very young. He liked the swimming pool and the squash courts and the steam room afterward. He and I spent lots of time working out there.

Jeff Ebner didn't care much that the ACC was "an example of Spanish Renaissance Revival with Italian influence" architecture, according to the club's website, or that to eat in the "formal dining room" he'd have to wear "business attire." To him, business attire meant a clean set of dress blues. Whenever he and Amy did eat in the dining room, he moaned about having to wear a sport coat.

The ACC opened in 1915. President Warren G. Harding was a member. So were Wendy's founder Dave Thomas and various senators and governors. The ACC is now what it was then, a place where rich guys in tailored suits meet to cut large deals. High ceilings, dark wood paneling, a place when you walk in, you start whispering.

We didn't have a lot in common with the clientele. It was an odd match for my dad's simple, eccentric tastes and his It's Fine substance. Truth was, we kind of resembled the Beverly Hillbillies hanging out by the cee-ment pond. It made for some interesting encounters.

The workout room was on the fifth floor. Lots of windows and people wearing Spandex. No one grunted. Except, of course, Jeff and Nate. We showed up in gray sweatpants or rugby shorts, Gold's Gym muscle shirts. My dad made headbands out of pieces of sponge, held to his head with rubber bands. They did the job. They were fine. He wore a pair of Adidas sneakers he found at a closeout sale, purple with yellow stripes, until the soles fell off. We'd bring our own chalk and belts and commence to slamming the weights on the floor like the ACC was the garage at the house on High Street.

People would get mad. They'd mutter and stare. My dad absolutely did not care. "If they don't like it, they can leave," he'd say. When someone gathered the nerve to complain to us directly, my dad would say, "Oh, did you pay for these weights?" Or, "I'm not pulling a muscle so I can gently set my hundred-pound dumbbells quietly on the floor."

Then blithely and purposely oblivious, he'd offer, "The weights will be fine. They're not made of glass."

When he was especially annoyed, my dad would pretend to be clueless about the commotion. "I'm sorry. I didn't realize . . ."

Then after his next rep, he'd slam the weights even harder.

He had other peeves. At a place epitomizing Spanish Renaissance Revival with an Italian influence, you'd guess he might.

Jeff Ebner hated it when people commandeered a bench, then sat on it between sets, when it was obvious other people (i.e., Jeff Ebner) were waiting. He'd almost go out of his way to make them feel uncomfortable, as they sat there with their headphones on, checking text messages on their phones.

"Can I use this machine?" he'd ask.

"I have two more sets."

"You're not doing them now."

Inevitably, the bench hogger would relent, but not without getting pissy about it. Where does that entitlement come from? Just share the space, OK?

The club did host some essential and historic squash matches between the two of us. Seven sets, Jeff Ebner standing in the center of the court, running his fourteen-year-old son all over the place. Even as I got older, I didn't win much.

I spent half my youth trying to take family records from him. Rowing was a prime example. My dad was very proud of his rowing personal best: seven minutes and one second for two thousand meters on the machine. At age forty-five.

That family mark stood until my 2019 off-season. I could have done it sooner, I think, but I'd have had to go to a dark place to do it. I was rowing a lot to get back in shape after a knee injury I'd suffered near the end of the 2017 season. I was feeling good, pulling 1:50 for 500 meters. Multiplied by four, that put me at seven minutes, twenty seconds, still nineteen seconds behind my dad's mark.

Then one day before a workout, I let it fly. I averaged 1:44 for 500 meters, which got me in at 6:56. New champion! Someday I will have to really blast it to see how low I can go.

I've adopted all my dad's gym behaviors, unfortunately, especially when it comes to slamming the weights and making people share the machines. I don't understand entitlement, and I don't put up with it. Even as a former member of the Patriots and the owner of three Super Bowl rings, I'm surprised at the adulation we receive as professional athletes. We're just people, excelling in a job lots of folks find important, for which we are paid lavishly. That doesn't make us better than anyone else, only more fortunate.

My dad saw himself casually. He took his work seriously, but not necessarily himself. He never was who he wasn't, no matter the situation. Our time at the ACC proved that. No one who got buck naked in a practice field parking lot was going to worry about what he looked like in a fancy workout room. My dad was at the ACC frequently. He wasn't of it. Workout, squash, steam room, leave.

He did spend a few New Year's Eves there with Amy, mostly because the club had a few bedrooms that members could use.

He liked to get his celebratory smashes in (metaphorically speaking) knowing he didn't have to drive and could sweat out the alcohol the next morning.

I THINK OF OUR TIME at the Athletic Club of Columbus the same as I do all of our time together. When I think of my dad slamming the weights on purpose, I smile. That was him.

It was a regular thing—we'd meet at the ACC a couple times a week after my last class, work out together, then eat. It was no different from our weeknights together in Mason, when I was younger, except for what we talked about.

I knew Jeff Ebner would support any decision I'd make. I knew, too, that he'd express his feelings on the subject, which would make me think more deeply about my own. There was no one else I'd rather have shared my decision about football with.

I explained my thinking: A professional rugby career wasn't going to work. I could always go back to rugby— in fact I never considered that I wouldn't. I wanted to play in the NFL and would use Ohio State as a jumping-off point. I never told anyone outside my immediate family about my NFL plan until it became obvious my senior year.

There was never any question that the first person to whom I'd tell my cockeyed dream would be my dad. The What in Jeff Ebner's life was me. That was bedrock for me. What's not so obvious is the Why. My dad moved the world on my behalf. Why was he so lovingly urgent about it? When my dad was ten his parents, Dick and Lyla, divorced. Lyla and their two children, Jeff and Jill, moved from Springfield, Ohio, to Cleveland, where Lyla had grown up. Eventually, Lyla remarried and the new family moved to Minnesota. Dick stayed in Springfield, to run the junkyard, and eventually also remarried.

What happened for the next decade is the messy stuff all families endure. Even families whose members love one another very much. We all have a past and we all have a family, and neither is spotless. Even the best family photo comes with a thumbprint in the corner of the shot.

My dad and his dad didn't see each other for long stretches. Jeff grew up in Minneapolis, graduated from high school in 1973, and attended Drake University on a football scholarship. After his third year there, he transferred back home to the University of Minnesota, where he graduated with a degree in history. Minnesota is also where he picked up rugby.

My dad wanted to become a lawyer. He even took the LSAT. Instead, as I mentioned, he took a job in Dallas with Electronic Data Systems, the legendary firm founded by H. Ross Perot. But Jeff longed for a relationship with Dick, his birth father. Lyla and her husband, Harvey, had given Jeff and Jill a good life, but Jeff felt an emptiness known by young children who have lost their parents, either through death or forced separation. As an adult, he wanted to recapture something he'd had taken from him.

Jeff was in his midtwenties in about 1980, when he quit his job at EDS and went back to Springfield. He would help his dad run the yard and resume a relationship he'd feared he'd lost. My dad liked working at the yard. It was his kind of toil, and the flexible hours allowed for his rugby passion. Jeff and Dick Ebner succeeded in making up for lost time. They became great friends and coworkers.

My dad and I didn't talk much about any of it. He didn't bring it up, I didn't ask. It wasn't relevant to our day-to-day. We had our life together. That's all that mattered. I don't have a degree in psychology, so I can't tell you for sure how my dad's forced estrangement from his dad affected how he treated me. I can only guess Jeff Ebner saw his past and vowed it would not become my future. I think he invested himself in me because it brought him joy.

When my dad and my mother divorced, my mom knew he was a good father, and she told him he could see me whenever he liked, and that's exactly what he did. History would not repeat itself. Jeff and Nancy were the gold standard of divorced parents: friendly and respectful. My mom was generous, my dad was grateful. I was cocooned securely in the middle.

Families can be strange associations, even when divorce is not involved. It took a lot for my dad to leave a promising new career in Texas, to take a shot at a meaningful relationship with his birth father. That was the man he was.

Now here I was at dinner telling my father that I wanted to turn my back on the sport he loved so much, the sport that had done so much to bring us together, in order to pursue what had to seem like an unlikely dream. Jeff Ebner knew rugby was a professional dead end for an American who didn't want to leave the country, but he wanted to be sure I understood the consequences of what I was attempting.

"I don't want you to give up everything you've done in rugby. You've created a path for yourself to play professionally. You're going to give that up just to play football at Ohio State?"

I told him about my NFL dream.

He didn't blink. "Commit to it. Don't play just to say you played football at Ohio State," my dad said. He knew I'd never do that. He was just making sure. "If you're going to do it, you gotta be all in. No regrets."

No regrets. With that I was in: I would walk on, find a way to get on the field and do well enough to attract the attention of NFL scouts. I would get my pro chance. I was sure of that. Even if almost no one else was.

There was other motivation. In Ohio, Ohio State football isn't just a passion. It's not a cult, either. It's way too big and mainstream for that. It's a way of life, a touchstone. Part of what makes Ohio Ohio. When you say you're from Ohio, people assume you root for the Buckeyes. If you actually play for the Buckeyes? You're a god. Unofficially, of course. Except on Saturdays between September and January. Then, you are officially a god.

I wanted to know what it felt like to be part of that. An official god of Saturday afternoons.

It helped that when I went public with my intentions, everyone—I mean everyone, except possibly my mother and later my trainer Butch Reynolds—told me I was crazy. I had a lot of people rooting for me, but almost no one believing in me.

When I told Ron Bowers I was walking on, he said, "You're a phenomenal athlete, an all-American rugby player. But Ohio State has 120 guys like you." This from someone I played with and for. A guy who coached me. Who *knew* me. And he's saying this stuff.

My stepfather, Doug Paplaczyk, was and is a Buckeye football obsessive. The basement of his and my mother's home in the Columbus suburb of Dublin was a shrine to his obsession. Doug told me he had his doubts.

What was more prevalent and just as annoying were the students, some of them friends, who either patronized me or thought I was joking. I can't tell you how often I heard how great the football players were, followed by "Wow, Nate, you didn't even play in high school?"

"Dude, you might be a good rugby player, but you could never play football at Ohio State. If you even made the team, you'd never get in a game."

Every doubting comment was kindling for my fire. I'm not one ever to say "I told you so." That doesn't mean I don't think it. I don't need external motivation—I'm my own motivation—but I'd be lying if I said my doubters never helped me get through a crushing workout or a mind-numbing film session.

Ohio State football players were people, just like me. They were gifted, sure, but I was gifted, too. Maybe not to their five-star, blue-chip levels, but I was sure that whatever I lacked in skills or measurables I would overwhelm with my sweat ethic. It had never failed me before.

My dad and I never asked why. We always asked why not. Sometimes, the why-nots were outrageous. Most of the time, the why-nots nested comfortably within our outstretched arms. *Other people are doing this. Why can't we?*

My dad and I never expressed that we were special. We just knew we were. We expected it from ourselves. Always, the proof was in the doing, not the talking. My mom said it best: "Nate thinks highly of himself. He just doesn't want you to know he thinks highly of himself."

Above all, I needed to answer one question: What can I achieve when I give it everything I have? I asked myself, *What am I capable of? Why should I let others make that call? They've never spent a day in my shoes or a weekend in my dad's junkyard. Why should I let them define me? I can control the outcome with my effort and attitude.* I was sure of this.

Every year that Ohio State beats Michigan, each Buckeye player gets a pair of gold pants. In the Dark Ages, when Michigan actually was competitive with Ohio State, the OSU coaches would tell their players, "Michigan's players put their pants on one leg at a time, just like you guys." Hence the gold pants to mark wins over what Woody Hayes referred to as "That Team Up North." I took that same mindset with me into the walk-on workouts.

My dad and I left the ACC knowing I was making my own decision and fully owning its consequences. I knew he had my back no matter what. That meant everything to me.

The next day, November 13, 2008, Jeff Ebner was working late at the junkyard when a robber jumped him from behind and smashed his head in with a piece of pipe. Jeff Ebner died the next day.

IT'S POINTLESS AND IMPOSSIBLE to describe what it felt like to lose my dad. Pointless because, although I think of him every day, sometimes all day, I can't bring him back. There's no future to conquer if you're anchored to the past. Things go wrong, sometimes indescribably wrong, but they are things you cannot change. So you move forward to what's next. The quicker you can do that, the more success you will have, be it the next play on a football field or the next phase of your life. This doesn't mean denying your grief; it means the opposite, something much harder: picking up the heavy load of your grief and carrying it forward with you.

My dad spent my lifetime nudging me along, one bench-press rep at a time. Forward was the only direction he knew, or allowed. Jeff Ebner left the earth knowing what we meant to each other. What I'd like him to understand, somehow, is that everything I have done and will do is to honor his memory and make him proud of the son he raised.

I will not mention the name of my father's killer. He was a lowlife, little different from any other lowlife who tried to steal from us. We'd have dealt with him the same way we dealt with the others, had he not attacked my dad the cowardly way he did. We'd have applied a little citizen's justice, made another independent arrest. Chances are, we'd never have seen him again.

The guy had bought a used car from us earlier in the day. It was a wreck. He drove it off the lot, but later it died and couldn't be revived. This isn't unusual when you buy a car from a junkyard. He came back to Ebner's wanting his money back.

My dad was on all fours under a lift, working on his truck. He told the guy to fuck off. "You bought a car from a junkyard," I could imagine my dad telling him. "You knew there was a chance it wasn't going to work." The guy left pissed off.

He came back not long after, with a couple buddies and a piece of pipe, and he started swinging. I don't know exactly what happened. I don't like to think about it. It doesn't change anything. The guy hit my dad in the back of the head. From behind. A gutless act. My dad was found to have a broken arm, so he must have tried to defend himself.

My grandfather had left for the day. I called the yard at four p.m. I'd just finished a workout and wanted to tell my dad about it. No answer. An hour later, my aunt Lani called me. "Nate, there has been an accident. Your dad's in the hospital." I thought he'd been in a car wreck. He wasn't a great driver. Anyone who'd watch a movie while wearing headphones and navigating an interstate wasn't a good driver.

I jumped in my car and drove ninety-five miles an hour to the hospital. When I saw him, I knew it wasn't a car crash. One of his eyes was swollen shut. A tube that resembled an antenna ran from the side of his head to a machine next to the bed. It monitored the swelling in his brain. He had a partly fractured skull. He was in an induced coma.

After a while, I drove back to Columbus for the night, figuring my dad would be in for a long recovery and guessing he might never be the same, but grateful he was alive. I put my cell phone on silent. When I woke up, I had thirty missed calls. I hurried back to the hospital. My dad's brain swelling had increased overnight. He never regained consciousness. He died from brain trauma, at age fifty-three.

News and police reports said my dad was found with $800 in cash in the pocket of his shirt. Police said they were alerted by an anonymous 911 call that the murderer admitted he'd made. He was charged with aggravated murder, two counts each of felonious assault and aggravated robbery and one count of tampering with evidence.

He pleaded to one count of murder and was sentenced in July 2010 to fifteen years to life in prison. He has a possibility of being paroled.

I'll never be paroled. Nothing will relieve me of the sadness of missing my father, and the absolute bittersweetness in knowing that everything I accomplish, I will never be able to share with him. My wins are his wins, only he's not here to witness them. There is no parole from that.

In those first few months after he died, I wasn't thinking about any of that. I was thinking about how I'd get through the day. More times than I can recall, I'd think of something important, then tell myself, *I'll have to ask my dad about that.* And then realize I couldn't. Not ever again. To this day, I will have the reflexive urge to call him when I have a problem or a triumph that needs sharing. I'll reach for my phone, then just as quickly pull back my hand. If you can come up with a description for the feeling that provokes, let me know. It has been twelve years. I still can't explain it.

All I can do is everything I can to stay true to what he hoped for me. The last thing I told him was that I was going to walk on at Ohio State, with an eye on getting an NFL shot. It was time to start making good on that vow.

NINE

"Live a Life He'd Be Proud of"

After my dad died, I dropped out of Ohio State for the rest of the quarter. I tried to return. My first week back, I sat in an anthropology class where the professor talked about cavemen killing each other with blunt-force weapons. I walked out and didn't go back.

I went home to my mom's house in the Columbus suburbs and shut down completely for six weeks. Spiritually, I was on life support. For nineteen years, I'd had a wind at my back and now everything was still. The rock I'd leaned on was gone. I spent most of every day playing video games in the dark, a hoodie pulled tightly to the tops of my eyes.

It's funny. When I was at Ohio State, my dad and I would meet for workouts at the Athletic Club of Columbus. Afterward, we'd have some dinner, then get in our cars and go our separate ways. We'd both take I-70 West to I-270, where I'd exit and he'd continue on to Springfield.

The land around Columbus is completely flat, so after I exited I could watch his taillights as he drove down I-70. I'd always wonder, *Will this be the last time I see my dad?* It was strange and irrational thinking. And then it wasn't.

To fight the pain, I needed more pain. Specifically, the singular ache of working out until I was beyond exhausted. Workouts were already as much a part of my life as breathing. I enjoyed waking up and figuratively setting my body on fire. When my body was screaming at me, I embraced it. It hurt bad. It felt good. At least I was feeling something.

It was more than that, though. Exercising made me feel closer to my father. Everything had changed. But when I was squatting and dead-lifting and taking my body to its edge, I could pretend that a few things had not changed. My mother and stepfather saw me torturing my body in their basement, and they asked me to tone it down. They worried for my well-being.

What they didn't understand, what nobody could understand, was that working out made my life tolerable. The memories of my dad, the lessons he taught. The time. That was our time. I'm not an overtly spiritual or religious person. But the weight room was our temple.

I was supposed to be preparing for this football dream with my dad at my side. *Finish strong, Eb.* He was supposed to be with me, urging and cajoling, my partner and my conscience. My best friend, riding shotgun on this quest.

Everywhere I looked, he wasn't there.

It wasn't just our workouts I needed, though they painted the best portrait of who we were together, and what we meant to each other. *Only the great ones can take the pain, Eb.*

It was the two-hour round-trip drives he made during the week when I was in grade school and middle school, to visit me at my mom's house in Mason. Even if it was just for dinner. Or calling me every day, or flying by himself to Wales to watch me play rugby for the US Under-19 team.

All this, gone. For the only time in my life, I had no idea what to do, and little motivation to do it. I lived in this now-what? daze fueled by anger, fear, and sadness. I couldn't believe I'd never see my dad again. I could not wrap my head around this impossible nightmare.

Nobody who is nineteen thinks about mortality, theirs or anyone else's. Here was Jeff Ebner, fifty-three and ageless, a guy who could still beat me on the rower and give me a game on the squash court. He was my best friend and he was indestructible. Our story together was just getting started. Half the joy from my successes was in sharing them with him.

And now . . . what?

It wasn't just our past I thought of. No more "A-ight, later" to end a phone call. No more dinners at the ACC or laughs at the crazy stuff we'd done. *Dad, why did you make me cut our backyard with scissors?* No more rides home from rugby practice, dissecting our games. No more living our lives. That was bad. Worse would be all the times he'd miss. The times of my life that we'd worked for and would've shared. My first kickoff at Ohio Stadium and the day the Patriots invited me to play in the NFL. The moments before my first Super Bowl, quiet, grateful, contemplative. *We did it, Ebs.* A future without him around would never be as great as it was supposed to be. I knew the memories would be eternal. I couldn't yet know the haunting would last just as long.

Years later, I know my dad is with me. But I can't see him, hug him, laugh at something goofy, or shove him the fat from my steak. It's a shaky peace I've made. Back in November 2008, there was no peace.

I'd thought about going to the junkyard and just beating people up. Seriously. Not solely for that purpose. I was thinking of my dad. Maybe I'd stop at the junkyard, talk to my grandpa Dick Ebner, who still worked there every day. I half hoped somebody was doing something sideways when I got there.

I'd drive toward Springfield, thinking dark thoughts, get halfway there, then turn around, thank goodness. I don't know what I might have done had I actually reached Ebner & Son. Nothing good.

MY MOM, NANCY PRITCHETT, let me hide inside myself for several weeks. She knew more than anyone what Jeff Ebner had meant to me. But eventually, she'd had enough. My mom couldn't stand watching me ignore life any longer. It was around my twentieth birthday, December 14.

"Nate, I have to talk to you," she began.

She'd been thinking for days about what she would say, and the touch with which she'd say it. She didn't want just to say, "It's time to get on with it." She knew that no kid should have this happen. She knew that my father had become my best friend.

She also knew that excusing my behavior forever might ruin my life, and everything my dad wanted for me. So she said the following, and I remember every word:

"You cannot continue to live like this. I know you lost your dad. No one feels more sorry for you than I do. But he wouldn't want to see you throw your life away because he's gone."

I didn't say anything. My mother wasn't seeking a conversation. "You need to live a life he'd be proud of," she concluded.

I listened. I could see how hard this was for her. She wore it on her face. I'd never seen her cry that way. It struck me how much strength it took for her to muscle those words out. She shook as she spoke.

If anyone else had said the same things, I wouldn't have listened. My mom's was the only qualified voice.

She could have coddled me. A mother's protective instinct might have kicked in. She could have continued to enable my defeatist behavior indefinitely. She knew that ultimately, that behavior was pointless. She made me look my dad's death straight in the face and deal with it the way he'd have wanted.

My dad would have summed it up this way: "Fuck it. We're all gonna die. At least I didn't go in a wheelchair."

If Nancy had let me wallow, I'd have had a built-in excuse for every failure in my life.

I knew another person who had lost his father early on. His mother hugged him and rationalized his misbehaviors. The former Nancy Ebner would not do things that way with me. No rationalizing bad behavior. If ever the seed were planted for me to live the life my dad prepared me to live, that was the moment. It was more than a little conversation.

More than a decade later, I can still see her, struggling through tears to find the right words at a time when the right words desperately mattered. Not to get over it. That will never happen. But to get on with it. The more time I've had to think about what my mother said, the more I've recognized the courage it took. It was one of the most important moments of my life.

My dad was the cofounder of my spirit. My mom relit it. She was the one who set me straight, when getting straight was everything. I had a life to live, and I would dedicate it to making my dad proud. She would say that she was only being a good parent. That shortchanges her role. She could have done what was easy. She did what was hard.

I had a month before walk-on workouts at Ohio State. I called Butch Reynolds, asked him if he'd train me. Butch was an Ohio guy. He'd won a gold medal at the 1988 Olympics, as a member of the four-by-400-meter relay team. He held the world record in the 400 meters for eleven years and won an Olympic silver medal in the event at the '88 Summer Games. He had parlayed his international track success into a job as OSU's speed coach. He'd just left that job when he worked with me and a Scioto Valley teammate, Kevin Mongold. Butch hoped that training us would give him an in with the national Men's Sevens rugby team.

The walk-on tryout at Ohio State was January 14. I needed to be faster and more explosive for the measurables the coaches would clock. I didn't know a thing about football workouts. Only that if other guys could survive them, I could, too. As my dad had said more than once, "They're human beings, you're a human being. If they can do it, why can't you?"

TEN

Walking On

A 2019 NCAA study showed that 2.8 percent of high school football players go on to play Division I college football, and the odds of a kid who played high school football getting drafted by the NFL were nine in ten thousand. That's .0009 percent. There are no numbers for players like me, who didn't even play high school football. Those chances are so slim, no one has ever bothered to quantify them.

I wasn't attempting to walk on just anywhere. In the past decade, only Alabama has signed more blue-chip football players than Ohio State. Walk-ons almost never play on Saturdays. They're scout teamers, used to simulate the opponent's offense or defense. The Buckeyes suit up 120 players every week. Between 55 and 60 actually get on the field. The others are what my dad would call "fodder."

At Ohio State, fodder guys run scout team all week, wearing beat-up jerseys bearing the colors of the next opponent. They do the same workouts everyone else does, go to every practice and meeting and weight-lifting session. And play about as much as Brutus the mascot.

A few do play special teams, but not with an NFL career in mind. As of May 2019, OSU has had forty-nine players drafted since the Patriots chose me in 2012. They all came to the university on scholarship.

Those were the odds I faced when I met with Butch Reynolds in early December, to train for the one-day walk-on tryout.

I had this promise I'd made. It was a burden and a joy. I walked around with this refrigerator strapped to my back, and it felt good. It was a comfort, a motivation, an essential purpose. It was also heavy, and it would only get heavier. I've never been freighted with thoughts of What If? But this time, I didn't know what I didn't know. I was walking blind into the hardest workouts of my life to that point.

I liked to be told I couldn't do things. I couldn't have been more than three or four years old when I told my mom I wanted to be a football player when I grew up. She said that was great, but I should probably have a backup plan. It made me mad she would think that way.

I didn't walk on at Ohio State just because people doubted I'd make the team. I didn't need that motivation. Besides, motivation is temporary. It's a spark. A pregame speech, a fiery teammate on the sideline, a newspaper story on a bulletin board. Just a flicker. I measured myself against my own expectations. Walking on was about conviction and keeping a promise. Crushing the perceptions of people who didn't know me was icing on the cake.

Butch and I set to work. The object was to lower my time in the forty-yard dash. I knew they'd be timing us in the forty at the walk-on tryout. I wanted to play safety. I needed the speed training. I also needed the accountability of showing up every day to train.

I didn't have much time. Ohio State used the walk-on workout to find players who were athletic enough to hang with the scholarship guys. Close to eighty aspiring football players showed up. A few quit during what coaches called the "dynamic warm-up," a fifteen-minute, high-energy stretch. Many more exited as the tryout progressed. Some of these walk-ons had played high school football. All thought they wanted to be part of Ohio State football. It worked much better for them as a concept.

I ran forty yards in 4.5 seconds, on cramping legs. Thanks, Butch. At the end of that session, coaches picked me and fourteen others to move on to walk-on workouts for the next two weeks. We were still isolated from the rest of the team. Their goal was to separate the serious players from those who just wanted to wear the jersey.

Only the 2016 Olympic rugby selection camp was more of a

physical grind than the walk-on workouts. The walk-on work-outs were insanely hard. There is no players association to monitor the proceedings or to ask they be toned down. When coaches said they wanted to know if we were willing to die to become Buckeyes, they were only half joking. Every session in the weight room or on the indoor field made me question what I was doing. Three workouts into it and I was thinking, *I have another ten days of this?*

In the long run, it didn't matter. There was nothing physical you could put me through that I couldn't handle. Nothing could feel worse than losing my dad. And I had too much riding on the outcome. I actually enjoyed waking up every morning to set my body on fire with pain. I felt alive. I embraced that.

The workouts were medieval. We did walking lunges while lugging sixty-pound dumbbells in each arm. Fifty-three yards across the field, and fifty-three yards back. If any of the fifteen guys dropped a dumbbell, all of us had to start over.

My first try, I'm halfway across the field and someone drops a dumbbell. My second try, same thing. These aren't textbooks we're toting. They're 120 pounds of metal. I know this. It doesn't keep me from losing my mind every time someone drops one. I thought about how we were going to get through this.

Two of us managed to get across and back without anyone dropping a weight. We'd finish as fast as we could, then sprint back to help the other guys. "If you're going to drop a weight, rest it on your thigh," we said. "We'll help you." There was no rule stating a guy couldn't pass the weight off. He just couldn't drop it. These guys were shaking, their muscles were spasming. We held the dumbbells while a guy shook out his arms and legs. That's how we survived the walking lunges.

There were other trials. Timed bench presses, at 5:30 in the morning. How many can you do in a minute? Wall sits. How long can you last in a squatting position, your back plastered to the wall? I'd hold it for five minutes after a leg workout, hoping someone would notice I was the last man sitting.

Coaches mixed in sprints, too. Twenty half-gassers (across the field and back), consecutively, with thirty seconds rest in between.

The workouts validated the time my dad put in with me. Every garage workout, every run, every bike ride, every meter on the ACC rowing machine, they all got me through those fifteen feel-like-dying days. Jeff Ebner encouraged me, pushed me, urged me to get everything from myself that I could. I needed it all. I thought about him every idle second.

Things hurt, Eb. Life is hard. You don't just get to quit. Finish it out, as well as you can. Finish strong, or don't bother.

I refused to give in. My dad taught me to tap into myself. I could have been at the ACC, pulling on the rower, my arms and legs cooking in lactic acid, Jeff Ebner above me, urging, *Five hundred meters to go, Ebs. Can't stop now. It doesn't mean a thing if you don't finish. Finish strong.*

I could have been at the junkyard, draining a gas tank or tarring the roof on a ninety-five-degree day in July. *Cars don't crush themselves, Ebs . . .* I could hear his voice as clearly as the clanks from the weights I was lifting:

They're human beings, you're a human being. If they can do it, why can't you?

The tryouts were an initiation of sorts that, if you made the team, earned you a little respect. You belong here. You earned it. You're (marginally) one of us. They also got you the right to be disrespected full-time by coaches who had little time for you, and five-star peers who wanted the jersey number you were wearing.

I didn't care. I was there to make the team. I didn't need friends and I wasn't interested in small talk. Plenty of wannabes walked on for the fringe benefits: the status, the prestige, the women. Your weekends got a lot more interesting when you were a football player, even if you never played a down.

That didn't interest me. I tunneled in. From the day I walked on with eighty other hopefuls, football became a business. Nine months after my dad died, I remained in a cocoon of silence and focus. It would be another eighteen months before I emerged fully. I didn't want anyone's pity. And it was hard for me to have fun, knowing how much my dad would have enjoyed being part of my business plan. Everything was bittersweet, all the time.

Six of us made it through the workouts. Of the original eighty who walked on, three made the team. I was the only one who played more than a few snaps that fall. I earned a scholarship my senior year. I graduated in 2012 with a 3.5 GPA. Since then no walk-on from OSU has played in the NFL or been drafted.

Making the team was just the first step. Making an impression was an equally tough task. I might not have played a down of football in high school, but I had competed all over the world against the best young rugby players on the planet. I was nobody's fodder. It was up to me to change impressions. I didn't put in all that work to be some faceless guy in a beat-up practice jersey.

I might have been alone in that sentiment.

To coaches and teammates, I was "that rugby guy." Three years later, strength coach Eric Lichter would play a big role in preparing me for my pro day workout, before the NFL draft. In the summer of 2009, he was just another doubter. Lichter said I was "a confident nobody who decided to walk on to our football team."

"No kegs on the sidelines here," an assistant coach familiar with my rugby background said, early in spring practice. "No kegs at the World Cup, either," I shot back.

More wood on the motivational fire.

I need to make a distinction here. There are "preferred walk-ons" who get everything the scholarship players get, except the scholarship. These are invited walk-ons: They are recruited by the team to play. And then there are uninvited walk-ons, players like me, who are much more likely to remain invisible practice players.

Coaches looked through me like I was glass. "Good job, Nate. Now get outta there and let the starters get their reps." They didn't coach me the way they did the other guys. I wanted them to be on my ass and they weren't. I didn't figure to be part of their game-day plan. They had no time for me.

For two years, if I wanted to eat at the training table with the scholarship guys, I had to pay for it. My mother covered the cost, but not the indignity. A few weeks into that first summer camp, I'd gotten a little fed up with working my ass off and being ignored.

I walked into the office of Paul Haynes, my position coach, who himself had been a walk-on at Kent State. I said, "I don't care what you think. I'll find a way to get on the field." He chuckled at my nerve. Or my gall. "You might think that's funny now," I said. "I'm dead-ass serious."

I wasn't boasting. Smack me if I was arrogant. I was just more than a little frustrated. I felt disrespected. I thought I knew what I was doing, and what I was capable of. Nobody else seemed to think that, or was willing to take the time to look. They had to get the scholarship guys ready for the opener.

To this day, I have a chip about players who are given what I am not. Blue-chip recruits who arrive at Ohio State already higher on the depth chart than I am, high NFL draft picks blessed with favorable perceptions before they've earned them. That's even as I'm grateful for my experiences, and proud I've validated them. I will always be a blue-collar striver.

I played in every Ohio State football game for the next three years, on every kickoff, as a special teamer. My teammates voted me Most Inspirational my senior year. Also that season, coaches chose me to carry the American flag onto the Ohio Stadium field on the tenth anniversary of 9/11. The confident nobody inspired a lot of supposed somebodies.

More than anything, Ohio State gave me my life back. I needed something to divert my attention from my sadness and focus it on one task: to honor the last commitment I'd made to Jeff Ebner. I would make the football team. I would use it as a springboard for a shot at the NFL.

That promise "gave me a Why," as my friend and old workout partner Anthony Schlegel put it. It threw me into a fire that demanded I be present and with that, allowed me an escape from the constant drumbeat of my dad's memory, at least during the hours I was in the team facility.

When I worked out, I was able to remember Jeff and forget my sadness. Later, as I tried to absorb the classroom side of college football, I was so far behind that nothing less than total concentration would catch me up. I couldn't have daydreamed if I'd wanted to.

I was part of something bigger than myself. It's not cliché to say Buckeyes football is an enduring brotherhood. I might have gone through a harder initiation than most. That only made my membership sweeter. At that time, I desperately needed that connection to others who would hold me accountable. Life would go on and I needed to pull my head outta my hoodie and get on with it. The brotherhood did that for me. The team nature of football reinforced it. My teammates were counting on me, and I on them. My brooding did none of us any good. I'm not going to accept bitching from anyone else. Why should I accept it from myself?

Not long ago, my stepdad, Doug Paplaczyk, said, "I knew if

you made the team, you'd have a bunch of brothers. I wanted you to make it so bad. I thought it would save you."

It did. OSU football gave me a purpose and a reason. That's all I've ever needed. Over and over, football has proven to me that if I really want something, I can get it.

On September 5, 2009, I played in my first college game in an Ohio State uniform, against Navy. I made a solo tackle on a kickoff, in a game we barely managed to win. That was a sign of the struggles ahead for us that year.

ELEVEN

The Bracelet

I might have been attempting something audacious. Guys who didn't play high school football don't walk on at a place like Ohio State. But I didn't see myself as audacious.

I was a gifted athlete, though not as gifted as some. I was fast and strong enough that by the time I graduated, I was all over the OSU record board. Being on that board was one of my goals when I got there. I thought it would be a good way to get noticed. I had played rugby against the best young players in the world and held my own. I had a desire that I would put up against anyone's.

If audacity is defined in the dictionary as a "daring and willingness to take bold risks," then, yes, I was audacious at Ohio State. But after my dad died, I was playing with house money.

I knew true loss. I'd been to the darkest streets of my life, and I'd rediscovered the main road. How could not making a football team possibly hurt me more than losing my father? I could live with not making the team. My effort was genuine and complete. I busted my butt. I had every excuse in the world not to walk on at Ohio State.

If you're going to attempt the unlikely, you have to allow for the possibility you won't achieve it. I trusted myself and the way I was raised. I wasn't just a kid with a Laurinaitis jersey seeking the fringe benefits of being an Ohio State football player. I saw the unlikely successes I'd had already: collegiate all-American in rugby Fifteens as a freshman; a member of OSU's Sevens team, also as a freshman. I was on the US junior national rugby team, at sixteen, and I attended the US men's high-performance camp at seventeen. I played for Scioto Valley against men at the club nationals Sevens tournament.

Failure is in not making the attempt. It's a life spent wondering What If? This wasn't some small fork in the road. It wasn't a regret. A regret is wearing a T-shirt in a snowstorm. It was a decision that would impact the rest of my life. It would change everything. If my commitment and sacrifice are entirely present, what regrets should I have? Losing doesn't keep me up at night. I got tossed into this beast of a football operation and I had to find a way.

I thought my physical skills would lead me to start at safety for the Buckeyes. I couldn't have been more wrong.

The classroom work humbled me. I could tackle. I could run

and jump with the best players. But I didn't know what I was doing. I had no clue about the technical side of football. Football is the ultimate game of chess. I didn't even know the difference between man-to-man and zone defenses. Nickel and dime packages? What are those?

I was a weight-room warrior, but I didn't know a thing about playing college football. Conditioning was irrelevant if I couldn't be trusted on the field. I'd go to meetings hoping Coach Haynes wouldn't ask me to draw "21 Personnel, Pro-I Right" on the whiteboard. And that was a basic formation.

Formations. Personnel groupings. Football had its own language. So many terms: Mike linebackers who were Mack linebackers depending on the grouping. Formations with two backs and no tight ends or four wide receivers and no backs. This wasn't the Mason Comets peewees. This was a side of football for which I was completely unprepared. I didn't know shit about football. I wasn't giving the Xs and Os enough respect.

Nothing I'd done prepared me for Football 101. Rugby wasn't football. We had seven or fifteen guys on the field and aside from set pieces (lineouts, scrums, and tap penalties) we played on instinct, conditioning, and courage. There was no rugby playbook. It was more like a rugby pamphlet. We filmed practice at Ohio State, then watched the film right after practice to see all our mistakes. I never did that at rugby practice, on any level.

The last time I'd played football, I was fourteen years old. I saw a guy with the ball and I tackled him. On offense, they handed me the ball and I ran around everybody. The technical

"I'm still the champ"
is what my dad
would say.

Check out the headband and wristbands. At age three,
I already wanted to be just like my dad.

Chillin' in Florida, in my grandparents' pool.

Getting down to workout basics in the gym
behind the garage in Springfield.

MVP for the Mason
Comets, age eight.

On top of the world, skiing in
Aspen, CO, age thirteen.

We played
every sport.

Jeff "On Time" Ebner never missed my practices or games.

We went to a Tampa Bay Buccaneers game at Raymond James Stadium.
My first NFL away game as a player was in this stadium.

A rare shot of my dad and me all dressed up.

Jeff Ebner, playing rugby for the University of
Minnesota in the early 1970s.

My dad and Reecie the massive Rottweiler at the junkyard.
Reecie's kennel is in the background.

My dad and my
mother before I
was born.

My dad and Amy, his
second wife.

Mike Vrabel, then Ohio State's
defensive line coach, sharing a
special moment with me my
senior season, 2011. This was
my last practice at OSU.

Celebrating with my
Ohio State teammates
after a big special
teams play.

I carried out the flag on the tenth anniversary of 9/11.
One of my proudest moments in sports.

In the tunnel before a night game against the
Baltimore Ravens my rookie year.

Having a moment with my Patriots teammate Matt Slater, a seven-time Pro Bowler on special teams and one of my best friends in the game.

I'd just recovered a fumble in overtime against the Denver Broncos.
It resulted in a win for us, my second year in the NFL.

A collection of friends and family surprised me on my thirtieth birthday and stayed for the game at Gillette Stadium that Sunday night.

In 2019, my mom and stepdad, Doug Paplaczyk, helped me celebrate winning the Ed Block Courage Award, honoring one player on each NFL team who best exemplifies inspiration, sportsmanship, and courage. I got it for the work I'd put in rehabbing the ACL I tore at the end of the '17 season. I made it all the way back the following year, well ahead of schedule. The award was especially meaningful to me because the Patriots training staff voted on it. Cool trophy, too, my favorite.

Why we play this game.
My Super Bowl rings.
The most recent ring,
the one in the middle, is
ridiculously big.

Holding the Vince Lombardi Trophy, after the Patriots beat
the Los Angeles Rams in Super Bowl LIII, 13–3.

Chelsey and me at the ESPYs in 2017. They honored the Patriots for Comeback of the Year, in the Super Bowl against the Atlanta Falcons. We rallied from 28–3 down at halftime to win.

Chelsey and I got married in Ravello, Italy, in April 2019.

The rings given all members of the 2016 U.S. Olympic rugby team. We finished ninth overall at the Rio Games.

Before the U.S. team walked into Maracana Stadium for the Opening Ceremonies, we cooled our heels in a small arena just down the street. I wasn't especially thrilled with the team outfits. From left to right are my teammates Madison Hughes, Andrew Durutalo, Chris Wyles, Zack Test, and me.

In the midst of a Yaka Yard, hauling sand bags. Carlin Isles is with me, having lots of fun.

My former Ohio State teammates John Simon, left, and Brian Peters, supporting my Olympic effort while they're at NFL training camp with the Houston Texans in August 2016.

Grinding through a practice at Olympic training camp in July 2016.

I'm scoring a try against Fiji at the 2016 Summer Olympics. We lost in a close game. Fiji went on to win the gold medal.

Ringin' it at the Athletes Village in Rio de Janeiro, August 2016.

12·14·7

HAPPY B.D. - Nate

TO BECOME ELITE (BEST OF THE BEST)
ONE MUST OUT SMART; OUT TRAIN;
AND OUT PERFORM THE COMPETITION.

GO HEAVY OF DIE!

Jan.

Dad. Amy

B.D.
Nate - 12·14·7

YOU WILL GET
THERE!
DON'T QUIT.

Jan.

Dad.

Amy

During a recent move, I found these inscriptions
in two books from my father. They were the last
birthday gift he gave me.

stuff didn't get taught until high school. I was getting my rugby education in high school.

That's why I latched on to special teams at OSU. I knew I'd have a hard time ever getting looked at as a safety. Even if I mastered the ABCs, schools like Ohio State don't sign five-star safeties to sit the bench while they play a sophomore walk-on with no football experience.

The larger truth was, I didn't need to be a football scholar to play special teams. I had to tackle and be a little crazy. Running down the field and tackling the player carrying the ball isn't complicated. It's dog-eat-dog. From rugby, I already knew how to tackle. I liked tackling, and I loved playing with the crazed-dog attitude special teams requires.

It wasn't that I didn't study. I did. It wasn't that I would never understand the chess match. Eventually, I would. It was that I couldn't afford the time it would take to get smart. I needed to get on the field. That was the value in special teams.

I began to get noticed in practice, covering kickoffs. I'd get to the return man five or ten yards before anyone else. I knew I could turn heads with my effort, even as I was behind in my knowledge of the game. My first day of practice in the spring of 2009, I had to ask my lockermate how to attach my shoulder pads. Five months later, I was on the kickoff team against Navy.

I NEVER THOUGHT I was the "confident nobody" of Eric Lichter's description. I was no crash-test dummy. But it took me a few games before I wasn't invisible. That was partly my fault. I was still in what my friend Cody Blair described as "resting-bitch-face mode." I was hyperfocused on football, and when I'm that way, I can't be talked to. I was still angry about losing my dad and didn't feel like being social. I'm not a social being, anyway. I don't much like small talk.

When I'd hear people complain about trivial things, I literally wanted to grab them and shout, *Do you know my dad died when I was nineteen years old?! My best friend, my mentor, my protector. He was murdered. Did you know that?!*

Not to diminish their concerns. But maybe they hadn't experienced true loss. They were bitching about stuff they wouldn't remember the next day. For years after my dad's death, I'd grab my phone to call him. That's frustration. That's sadness. It's more than a bad day at the office.

I'm cynical about people in general. The more I live, the more I realize how full of crap people can be. How superficial. Too many people talk about what they're going to do, but don't sacrifice anything for it. They're hot-air frauds. I decided early on that I wouldn't be one of those people. When it came to football, I knew the pain of the game. If I saw the players around me digging as hard as I was, they got my respect. Underpromise, overdeliver. Stay humble about it.

I was getting noticed on Saturdays. I came out of my bitch-face hibernation, my shell, whatever you want to call it, late in October 2009, seven games into my first season. We lost at Purdue that week, 26–17, after falling behind 23–7 and committing five turnovers. This was beyond unacceptable. It wasn't Ohio State football.

The loss dropped our record to 5–2, not bad for most places, terrible for the Buckeyes. After the game, I met my mom at a wedding. Her brother Kenny was there. I mentioned that my teammates were taking the loss harder than I was. My dad's death had showed me there are things more dire than sports. Losing a game is temporary, something to learn from and overcome, not to mope about.

Kenny suggested I give all my teammates a bracelet.

They were black rubber, the words FINISH STRONG etched in white. My aunt Ann Bailin had sent me one eleven months earlier, after I'd eulogized my dad at his funeral. I tried to honor his memory with stories of the lessons he'd passed on. I finished by recalling a few words that will never leave me:

"Only the great ones can deal with the pain," he'd say. *"I know it hurts. Can you fight through it? That's the question. Ah-ight, Eb. Let's see what you've got."* And then it was up to me to finish strong.

Finish Strong is rooted in what my dad planted in me, a need to conquer what we set out to do and a duty never to turn away from anything because it was too hard.

We'd make a game plan for running hills—how many we'd run, how we'd run them—and we wouldn't deviate. Same with the gym, right down to the sets, the repetitions, and the pounds we'd be moving, all scribbled in the little black book. It forced on us an accountability to do exactly what we said we would.

That last set, those last few reps when everything in my body was begging me to stop. "Finish, Eb! Finish!"

As we got into more cardio training on the rowing machines or at the track—workouts that challenge you mentally and physically—it turned into "finish strong."

Finish Strong became a referendum on my character, will, and desire. Find what you really want and discover how badly you want it. Don't stop until you've gotten it.

I'd get on the rower and Jeff Ebner would stand next to me and talk me through 2,000 meters. A rowing machine is unforgiving. It can never be conquered, because the chances for better times are endless. We'd do 500-meter sprint intervals. During those last few intervals, my arms, legs, and back felt like molten lava. I'd be trying to hit times I'd reached before. My body wanted to lie down.

"Hold that pace, stay right there!" my dad yelled, to the rhythm of my pulls. Stay (pull). Right (pull). There.

At 250 meters: "OK, you passed halfway."

At 350: "Stay in the fight!"

At 400: "OK, Eb, finish strong now! You did all that work to get to this point, now you gotta finish!"

At 450: "Bring it home. RipItRipItRipIt!"

I'd finish that 500 meters, take a break and tackle the next 500. They became progressively harder. That's when my dad would ask, "What are you made of?"

These sessions taught me how to talk myself into going beyond what I thought was physically possible. That served me during those times when every muscle in my body was begging for mercy. I replaced my dad's urgings with my own. But they were always innately his.

Eventually, I started saying "start fast, finish strong" because you can't just bullshit your way through a workout, then finish strong. But the original exhortation never lost its power.

Uncle Kenny suggested that Aunt Ann order a few hundred more bracelets. I had them within a week. I asked Coach Jim Tressel the next day if I could talk to the team. I'd played in seven college football games. I hadn't said six words to anyone since I made the team. I was a walk-on, an undistinguished special teamer. That rugby guy. Tressel encouraged me to speak.

I wasn't comfortable doing it. I'm not a public speaker and the last thing I wanted was for anyone to feel sorry for me. But I did think my message was important and relevant, and in some small way, I wanted the respect of the room for the work I'd put in already, as a nonpreferred walk-on.

Players gathered in the Team Room. "My dad was murdered," I began.

I outlined my relationship with Jeff Ebner. I told them what finish strong meant to me. The message was this: *We can control what happens the rest of the season. We can't waste all the work we've put in. We can finish strong.*

It was the first time I allowed myself to be vulnerable about my dad's death. Everyone knew already I was dead-ass serious about everything I did. Now they knew why.

Eric Lichter remembered the speech: "We were awestruck.

The room was silent. Not just because it was a powerful presentation. The words were good, man. But Nate lived the behavior he was advocating. It resonated."

I asked my teammates to take a bracelet. I requested only they honor the words embossed on the rubber. It was too important to me simply to hand them out or stick one in every player's locker. "If you want one, just ask," I said. Players could come to my locker to get one. Almost every player did.

We won our last six games, including the Rose Bowl, and finished fifth in the country in the final Associated Press poll.

I put on that first bracelet in the fall of 2009. I've never taken it off.

I'VE SAID I CAN be motivated by being overlooked. I got plenty of that kind of motivation playing football at Ohio State. Even as a senior, after I'd advanced to playing on all four special teams units, I still faced moments of forced humility.

I was a senior when a freshman running back named Carlos Hyde asked to wear the number 34 I'd worn since I'd made the team. It wasn't a problem until late in the season. Hyde was on offense, I was a safety. The numbers on the field never duplicated. Then coaches put him on the kickoff return team. I was on the kickoff return team.

Did I mention I was a senior? And by then, a leader, an inspirer, and a very good special teamer. Not to mention Tressel had given me a scholarship the previous spring.

"Nate, can you switch numbers?" Luke Fickell asked. Fickell had been named interim head coach after Tressel resigned, in the wake of the Tattoogate disruption.

"Why?"

"Carlos wants to wear 34."

Son of a bitch.

"I'm a senior, he's a freshman," I said.

I didn't say what I was thinking, which was, *This is horseshit.*

I didn't get much response from Fickell. I had no ill will toward him. Fickell was in a tough spot. Five-Star Guy wants your number, Mr. Nonpreferred Walk-On. What are you going to do? I wasn't willing to fight over a jersey. I could have worn number 134, for all it mattered in the grand scheme. I was out there playing. I could hear my dad: *Eb, you're still gonna play, right? What does it matter?*

It was disrespectful. I'd proven so many people wrong by then, I'd earned a scholarship, and yet in some ways I was still that rugby guy. Sometimes, you welcome humility. It can be instructive and motivational. Other times, it's forced upon you.

I don't like to think playing special teams requires humility, because I believe special teams are as important to football success as offense and defense. But I understood that notion. When players bitch about playing special teams, they're worried about what people will think of them. To the insecure, being a special teamer is a stigma.

You don't have to be humble to be a good player on special teams. You don't see three-hundred-pound linemen on special teams. They're too slow. You will be humbled if you take the duty lightly. Ask any player who doesn't run hard and takes a block to the earhole on his way to the return man.

You have to be a dog. A dog is relentless. It understands that every second of every play is a fight. Nowhere in football is that more true than when you're covering kicks. You can't be soft on special teams.

There are places on offense for soft players to disappear, spots where they don't have to block or tackle. They can duck when they know a collision is coming. They can hide. There's nowhere to hide on special teams.

I loved the speed, the one-on-one battles, the collisions. Making tackles is my greatest joy in football. Flying down the field on a kickoff, beating all ten of my teammates to the return man and bringing him to the ground. To this day, the biggest adrenaline rush of my career came on the opening kickoff of my first college game. I jogged onto the field and a hundred thousand people were going nuts. I thought to myself, *I said I was going to play football at Ohio State and here I am. Anything gets in my way, I'm gonna blow it up.*

There is a delicate balance on special teams, between soft and reckless. Call it reasoned craziness. The best special teamers apply it to the controlled chaos they encounter. They know where the ledge is, and they respect it. Excelling on teams requires a certain amount of control. The best teamers can't be soft, either. If they are, they end up on their asses. In that way, it's a lot like rugby.

I pride myself on my tackling efficiency. In football as in

rugby, I don't miss many tackles. High-efficiency tacklers don't mind a head-on collision, but they also realize that sure tackling requires body control, not just speed. The returner isn't standing there waiting for you to jack him up. He's moving, too.

We developed a brotherhood on special teams in Columbus. We called ourselves the War Daddies. They called me Leonidas, after the Spartan warrior-king in the movie *The 300*. I was respected for the balls-out way I played. Hence, Leonidas. Warrior-king Nate.

Each special team had a military name. The kickoff return team was Delta Force, kickoff coverage was Recon. Rangers played on the punt return team. On kickoff coverage, they moved me around some, to wherever coaches thought I'd be most disruptive. I was often the R5, the inside guy on the right side, nearest the kicker. My job was to disrupt the return and make the returner commit to a direction.

When I was a senior, future all-American and NFL Pro Bowl linebacker Ryan Shazier was a freshman. He'd trail just behind me on returns. I'd either make the tackle, or on the rare occasion I missed, Shazier would unload on the guy.

I've never had an abiding love for special teams, other than a respect for what playing teams has allowed me to do. I do have an appreciation for special teams, though, and an understanding that most people (and players) lack. But special teams was never more than a means to an end for me. I could control my destiny playing on teams in a way I never could have as a safety.

At some point during my college career, I realized that special teamers in the NFL could play for a long and lucrative time. Core special teams guys made the roster year after year. That wasn't how I'd imagined my NFL future when I walked on in Columbus—humbled again—but I was able to adjust, modify, and adapt (another of my father's favorite phrases) to my circumstances, and thrive.

Over time, I earned respect for the work I put in, not because I started college football life as a five-star recruit. By the time I was a senior playing in the Gator Bowl, the University of Florida triple-teamed me on kickoffs.

From the opener against Navy, when our starting middle linebacker Brian Rolle became exhausted from playing his position and told our special teams coach, "I can't be running down the field on these kickoffs," to my last game as a senior, I had one purpose: to get noticed. First by my coaches, then by the head coach, and finally by NFL scouts. Sometimes, people have big goals and get sidetracked. I did not.

As a walk-on at Ohio State, I made a few arrogant assumptions and quickly had them humbled out of me. Other people made assumptions about me and were also humbled.

When something humbles you, you weren't giving it enough respect. Respect and humility are brothers. I learned that playing college football. My humility has had a prominent place in my success. I'm open to learning. I'm no better than the next guy, and I'm not too good to do anything. Remember, I worked in a junkyard.

TWELVE

Slaying the Selfish Beast

As iron sharpens iron, so a man sharpens the
countenance of his friend.

—PROVERBS 27:17

Iron and dirt. I didn't know any other way.

—ANTHONY SCHLEGEL

He was the Zen master of the Ohio State football weight room. My sensei. Not only did Anthony Schlegel understand my passion, he shared it. When it came to getting after it in the weight room, no one knew me better. Schlegel was a beast. He is a beast. In fact, he's an expert on beast.

Slay the selfish beast! Feed him to your inner beast! Then feed your inner beast iron! That was one of Schlegel's sayings. He wrote it on his weight belt. He had a few other sayings to motivate football players in the weight room—*Attack and Dominate!*—but Slay the Selfish Beast was the one I called on. Still do. It's Schlegel's version of Finish Strong.

I met him in 2010, my junior year at Ohio State, when Coach Tressel hired him as an assistant strength coach. Schlegel had been a member of the best-known group of linebackers in OSU history, a trio that included A.J. Hawk and Bobby Carpenter. The New York Jets picked Schlegel in round 3 of the 2006 NFL draft. He played two years in the league, but I think his true calling was in the weight room. The impact he has had on me is deep, maybe because we think so much alike.

The selfish beast is the voice in your head urging you to be average. That beast is an advocate of compromise. Its whispers urge self-satisfaction. *I've done enough for today.* If you listen to the selfish beast, you'll underachieve. You'll "cave in to the friction," as Schlegel put it.

Friction is life. Duties, obligations, weights on a bar. How you deal with friction tells you who you are.

The selfish beast never stops asking, *Is what I'm doing worth it?* It's not there when you start a workout, when the mental fight is a mismatch in your favor. It's easy when it's easy. The selfish beast appears when the bullets are flying and things start to hurt. When the lactic acid builds up and your lungs demand more air than your breathing can produce, the selfish beast comes to rest on your shoulder.

Your defense is your will. You marshal all the best clichés—

grit, heart, determination—and put them to work in your head, as servants of the inner beast. *Can I do this? Am I bigger than the task?* The inner beast has to answer yes. Yes to more training, because our growth depends on how hard we train. Yes to competition, because we surround ourselves with like-minded people to hold us accountable to our own high standard. No to everything else. No to pain, no to five reps when eight reps are required. No to settling. Settling is losing, in sheep's clothing. It's a nice way of saying, *I want this. But not badly enough.*

Lots of us say we "want" things in life. Few of us follow through. I like to think I'm one of those few. I feed my inner beast.

The inner beast is the rabid dog that won't let you stop. Obey that dog thoroughly enough and eventually, you get comfortable being uncomfortable. You crave the friction. The satisfaction in overcoming—silencing weakness with pure grit—is powerful and, for me, addictive. Letting that rabid dog go. There is no better feeling.

I'm sure all this sounds overly dramatic. Corny, even, until you've lived it. *Listen to Nate Ebner and his ten-cent philosophies.* But for me, Schlegel's mantra was pure sustenance. Walk-on workout day at OSU, my rookie year with the Patriots, and my desperate drive to make the Olympic Sevens team all demanded a high pain tolerance and an absolute refusal to lose to the selfish beast. I needed to trick my mind to do that.

Schlegel and I hit it off immediately. He was a grinder, he understood and respected the mission I was on. We were a lot alike.

He grew up in Texas, the son of a football coach who told him straight up, "We're blue collar and we work." Anthony was a ball boy and worked in the equipment room, attaching face masks to helmets. His dad first took him to the gym in 1991, when Anthony was twelve.

The way Schlegel tells it, the Metroplex gym was a refuge for serious lifters, a thirty-five-hundred-square-foot windowless warehouse where hard-core rap blared from the speakers and people attacked weights as if their livelihoods depended on it. Which, in a few cases (bodybuilders, powerlifters), they did. Basically, the Metroplex gym was the back of Jeff Ebner's garage, only bigger.

"Iron and dirt," was how Schlegel described the ambience. Places like that build muscles and a culture of grinding. "I didn't know any other way," he said. Neither did I.

I needed Schlegel's energy to supplement mine. Before I got to OSU, I worked out a lot by myself. I tended to wear other people out. I didn't need others around to motivate me, hold me accountable, or drag me down. At OSU, I could be outcompeted in the weight room. I had to bring my dawg to the fight every day, just to keep up with everyone else.

Schlegel and Eric Lichter ran the six a.m. lifting sessions. Schlegel didn't teach us how to lift. Eric Lichter did that. He was the mechanic. Lichter provided the How. Schlegel was the Why. Schlegel projected a sort of get-after-it charisma that affected almost all of us. He fed me energy. I put it to use.

Schlegel would say I made his job easier. No one wanted to

work out at six a.m. Everyone needed something or someone to get through it. To Schlegel, I was the someone. He could count on me wrecking it, every day. Getting in shape is about working, then pushing through when it gets hard. Nothing else. I'm good at that.

He and I also shared the belief that conviction begets greater conviction. Iron sharpens iron. The best workouts are with like-minded people. As Schlegel explained, "I want to surround myself with people that want to sharpen me 100 percent. That's what separates Nate from his peers with similar dreams. They don't want to be sharpened if it's uncomfortable. They didn't want the friction. Nate sought the friction. He took the path of most resistance. That's what I want."

Schlegel's workout ethic matched mine. He asked only for my best every day. His reason for working out was identical to mine. It wasn't to build beach muscles. Neither of us was interested in mirrors. Vanity didn't drive us; the beasts did. Overcoming our weaker natures was always the point.

Soon enough, our approach became contagious. Training beyond your comfort level is hard to teach and harder to do. Schlegel spread that gospel around the predawn weight room. If I led at all, it was by example. Schlegel didn't walk around the room telling players I was a walk-on. By then, they knew that, and they knew what I was about. He didn't say to scholarship players, "Ebner's a walk-on and he's beating you." I just did my thing. Sometimes, Schlegel paired me with players he needed to bring around mentally.

After I graduated and Schlegel resigned his position to start his own business, we'd still train together during my off-seasons with the Patriots. We valued authentic relationships that held us accountable, and people who'd say the things that needed to be said, with no agendas.

Schlegel got the use of the OSU baseball team's weight room, probably because no one else wanted anything to do with it. It was a dungeon. Small, funky, hot, a place the CIA might use to interrogate spies on weekends. "Let's get *swole*," Schlegel would say. At 5:30 in the morning, he'd crank the heat to 90 degrees and we'd slay some selfish beasts.

Working out is fun. Pain from working out tells me I'm about to have more fun, because I am going to defeat pain. Schlegel and I had a lot of fun.

He also trained Brian Peters. Peters was a Columbus-area native who played safety in college at Northwestern, another grinder who was never given anything. Peters wanted to be a linebacker in the NFL. That meant he needed to put on about twenty pounds. When Peters asked Schlegel to train him, Schlegel responded the way I'd guessed he might. "If you want to play linebacker professionally and you have a high give-a-shit factor, I will train you."

Peters was another piece of iron, more friction for me and Schlegel. Brian played four years in the Canadian Football League and four more in the NFL with the Houston Texans.

Schlegel was around when I was planning to tell Bill Belichick about pursuing the '16 Olympics. He asked me something I'd asked myself:

"If you didn't make the Olympics, or even if you did, and it meant you'd never play another down in the NFL, could you live with that?"

I could.

"Then follow your heart," Schlegel said. "Let's do what it takes to get you there."

Years later, he would add this: "Having the courage and conviction to follow through on what you believe in, we don't see that very often. Saying it's OK to have a dream and take a risk. That was Nate."

I STILL THINK ABOUT Schlegel all the time, because the selfish beast never goes away. Vigilance is the only defense. Pro Day workouts? One more L-drill, one more set of bench presses. Olympic tryout camp? One more sprint on dead legs, when my heart was wanting to escape my chest.

Not everyone is a slayer. It can be taught, though, and it doesn't require freakish athletic talent. Schlegel's words were as much a part of me as my arms or legs. Slay the Selfish Beast and Finish Strong were essential coconspirators in my effort to keep the promise I'd made to Jeff Ebner.

I showed up every day ready to attack it. Part of it was the promise. I wasn't going to let my dad down. But when you're talking about a process you live day in and day out for years, pushing your body to unreasonable places, the promise-keeping is not in the picture. It's all about who you are and what's inside.

Some guys didn't understand what Anthony Schlegel meant. I did. Completely.

I don't think we expect enough from ourselves sometimes, or from each other. We can be very accepting of our OK-ness. Schlegel never allows that.

The gym and the training are relatable to everything in life. You slay the beast. You dig deep, you overcome, you find a way. That's life, man.

THIRTEEN

Validation

J im Tressel is among the best people I've ever known. Tressel was the kind of coach who could make me consider joining that profession when my playing career is done. Tressel's sincerity could always overcome your cynicism. When he talked about "molding young men" on the football field, no one rolled his eyes. Tressel truly cared about his players. I will go to the afterlife believing he got a bad deal from the NCAA.

The memorabilia-for-tattoos scandal that came to be known as Tattoogate made my senior season a dysfunctional mess. The official version of what transpired in 2011 was this:

Between April and June 2010, Coach Tressel and a local attorney and former Buckeyes walk-on named Chris Cicero exchanged a flurry of emails. Cicero warned Tressel that several current players were trading Buckeyes memorabilia to a local tattoo parlor owner for cash and tats. The parlor owner, Edward Rife, was also a suspected drug dealer, Cicero wrote. Coach Tressel responded that he would take care of it.

That September, the coach signed the standard NCAA certificate of compliance, claiming he didn't know of any possible violations in his program. His contract with the school mandated a similar disclosure. Then, in December, the US Attorney's Office notified Ohio State that a raid of Rife's home and business produced Buckeyes memorabilia.

Coach Tressel told school officials he didn't know anything about that. He didn't mention the emails to and from Cicero. Later in December, the school talked to the six players involved, then declared each ineligible. Soon after, the NCAA suspended five of the players for five games each.

In January 2011, the university found the emails between Cicero and Coach Tressel. A month later, the coach admitted he knew the memorabilia-for-tattoos and cash was an NCAA rules violation. In May 2011, Coach Tressel resigned.

I like to think he had made the right people aware of the situation by word of mouth without a trail of evidence that would jeopardize the entire athletic department. University officials didn't want to suspend their star football players over some tattoos, at least not until it became public. When it did, there was no paper or email trail linking coach Tressel with university officials, so they were able to claim ignorance and sacrifice him to the NCAA lions. Whatever the case, the coach's biggest mistake was in trying to protect his players and straighten them out so their NFL chances wouldn't be affected. What was the worst thing you did when you were young?

The whole thing got out of hand quickly. Coach Tressel's players did stupid things and put him in a bad spot. He might have made some wrong decisions, but I believe he made them for the right reasons. And he paid a heavy price: he was forced to resign because of them.

That didn't wash away the considerable good Coach Tressel did. At camp each spring, he gave each of us what he called his Winner's Manual. It was a collection of quotes, from Gandhi to Tiger Woods. "Read what you want," Tressel would say.

The manual was useful to some guys, to channel their minds, get the bullshit out. You're tired, you're bored, you're a little beat up? Read some Manual. Learn about some people who understood their purpose in life, and lived it. Tressel set aside "Quiet Time" for the reading.

The season itself was not good. Tressel resigned before the season. Luke Fickell, the defensive coordinator, had the thankless task of being interim head coach. Terrelle Pryor, our quarterback and a player at the center of the scandal, skipped his senior season. Nothing went right. We ended up 6–7, the only Buckeyes team in twenty-three years to finish with a losing record. I thought the scandal was overblown and forced my coach to take the fall. The NCAA didn't ask for my opinion.

. . .

THE ONLY CONSTANT FOR me my senior year was my focus. The previous off-season, I'd attended the pro day workouts for the seniors, to give myself an idea of what I'd be up against in twelve months. First, I had a senior season to play. The six months between September and my Pro Day in February 2012 would be the most important of my life. They'd represent everything I was about and every promise I'd ever made to myself and my dad.

It started with the flag. We played Toledo on September 10, 2011, one day short of the tenth anniversary of the terrorist attacks on the Pentagon and the World Trade Center. Coaches had to decide which player deserved the honor of running onto the field during pregame, carrying our flag in remembrance.

"There was no need for a vote," Fickell recalled years later. As Anthony Schlegel put it, "Nate represents what the flag represents. Attitude and effort. Spillin' it, all the time. His life and body of work deserved that honor." I was incredibly moved and humbled.

September 10, 2011, was a beautiful day in Columbus. It was late-summer pretty, the sort of weather that makes you wish late summer would last forever. Just before noon, Coach Fickell and I stood shoulder to shoulder in the tunnel behind the south end zone. I propped the flag on my shoulder pad.

I was familiar with 106,000 people going crazy in unison. This was Ohio State, and we were playing football. What I heard that day was beyond that. Fans had a second agenda, to fill Ohio

Stadium with gratitude. Their mindfulness sounded like a moon rocket launching at midfield. Every single fan was cheering for the flag and what it represented. And I was the one holding the flag.

I ran the length of the field. I got to the opposite corner and just stood a minute, waving the flag while the fans lost their minds. Cheering me, cheering OSU football. Cheering our country. I've never experienced anything like it.

This was what validation felt like. Pride mixed with satisfaction, supplemented by overwhelming gratitude. I didn't need that sort of affirmation from anyone but myself and my father, and my father wasn't around. I never answered the skeptics with anything but my actions. They were always sufficient. This was different. I stood there and let the moment own me.

Carrying the flag was humbling on a big, majestic scale. My work ethic mattered, and not just to me. It was more than that, though. The flag and the national anthem go together. I've stood hundreds of times, maybe thousands, for our anthem. I've heard it all over the globe. In Scotland and Wales as an Under-19 rugby player, in front of almost no one. At the Super Bowl, Beyoncé singing, in front of the world.

It's never less than powerful for me, a privileged moment I use to reflect on how far I've come and how grateful I am. We don't do many things as one in this country. For me, "The Star-Spangled Banner" is one of those things. We're rightly proud of our individualism and the freedom to express it. That shouldn't prevent us from coming together for a moment of grateful silence or singing. You'll always see me standing.

Nowhere else on the planet but the United States would my story go the way it has. I don't know of any other country where my great-great-grandfather could show up on its shores in 1883, not speaking the language, not knowing where to go, and start a business that still exists.

That is uniquely American. I believe I am uniquely American. I validate a cherished belief about our country, one that still has immigrants seeking our dream: In America, if you work hard, anything is possible.

With every day that passes, with every new experience I have, I understand more what a moment that was, what a singular opportunity I was given to represent something far greater than myself.

By my senior season at Ohio State, I was special teams captain. I'd figured out how to play teams. The physical side of it came naturally. I could run, I could tackle, I had no fear. The mental aspect wasn't as taxing as playing offense or defense, but there were techniques and strategies I had to learn to be the player I needed to be to get an NFL chance. There were guys who could run fast and through a wall of blockers, but they didn't make tackles. That's where technique played a part. Very good special teams players understand the leverage needed to move an opponent the direction they want him to move. They know when to engage a blocker (or make a block) and when to disengage. You don't run around blocks. You don't get glued to blocks.

My position coach, Paul Haynes, asked me that turbulent season to become a team leader. I felt I led by example. I was consistent, I was on time, I never took a moment off. I lived the saying embossed on the bracelets I distributed my first year with the team. But Haynes asked me to be more vocal about it. I wondered how that would work, given I didn't play offense or defense. "You want me to be a leader, but you won't play me," I said.

That argument didn't work. I played three snaps my senior season.

I couldn't tell you what impact my leadership had, if any. Certainly not as much as losing four senior offensive stars because of Tattoogate. Pryor threw for twenty-seven touchdowns the previous year and ran for four more. He withdrew from school and didn't play a down in 2011. Running back Dan "Boom" Herron and wideout DeVier Posey had combined for twenty-three TDs in 2010. The NCAA suspended each for five games in 2011; they had five touchdowns total that year. Mike Adams was a starting tackle who went on to play four seasons in the NFL.

Fickell appreciated my dedication. In a crazy year, he valued my steadfastness. He said he leaned on me. I remained the six a.m. workout warrior. Turmoil or not, I was still chasing a bigger goal.

My weight-room work-itude might have made an impact. I know it made the coaches' lives easier. They relied on me to get after players who weren't pushing their potential. They paired me with guys they wanted to bring around. They knew I set a high standard for myself. I knew what it meant to train beyond my comfort level. I tried to share that knowledge by example.

Working out at six in the morning isn't fun. It's designed to sharpen a mindset. It's dark, it's cold, you're working on five hours' sleep because of the studying you did the night before. You still have the whole damned day to navigate.

How badly do you want this? How much do you want to be great? What are you willing to do, and to what lengths are you willing to go, to do it? My first year on the team, the upperclassmen would see this walk-on special teamer beating everyone's ass and it would motivate them.

Nearly a decade later, Luke Fickell said I inspired him. "The program had no energy," Fickell said. "I knew Nate could provide it. I leaned on him to energize me."

I DIDN'T HAVE TIME to dwell on the might-have-beens. I'm not wired that way, anyway. I'd devoted three years to doing everything I could to keep a promise. One down year didn't skew that tunnel vision. My pro day was next. After we ended the year with a loss in the Gator Bowl, I had six weeks to train. I thought playing three years at OSU was an accomplishment. It was only the beginning.

Pro Day is an audition, especially for those players not invited to the Scouting Combine, the meat-market workouts conducted in Indianapolis each February, a few weeks after the NFL season. It's also a second chance for players who didn't test well at the combine. I wasn't asked to the combine. That was for better-known players, not confident nobodies.

NFL scouts gather on campus for one day of testing. Running, jumping, lifting weights, the ability to change direction. What the NFL calls "measurement testing." Stopwatches, measuring tapes, scales, cones, et cetera. Things that told coaches everything about a football player except if he could play football.

I didn't question it. For me, Pro Day was everything. I'd come into my own on special teams, and I had decent video for coaches to evaluate. I went to a pedigreed football school. Coaches who looked beyond my résumé found the intangibles on which I'd based my athletic career.

And yet . . .

Pro day wasn't about intangibles. I'd played just three downs of college football.

Most NFL special teamers were starters in college. I ended my college career in the Gator Bowl, where Florida triple-teamed me on kickoffs. But the distance between the Gator Bowl and the Super Bowl is impossible to measure. I needed to kill my Pro Day.

For six weeks, five days a week, four hours a day, I trained with Eric Lichter, the OSU strength coach. Lichter did his best work preparing players for their Pro Days.

Before he took the Buckeyes job, Lichter trained pro athletes in his gym in Cleveland, among them LeBron James. In a decade at that job, before he sold the business, Lichter trained twenty-two first-round draft picks, NFL and NBA. He knew what the NFL scouts wanted to see. Lichter's workouts centered on explosive movement. Very detailed, hands-on training geared specifically to acing the measurables.

Lichter didn't train players who didn't have reasonable NFL goals. I had teammates who all but assumed they'd play professionally, from the time they walked on campus: Posey, Herron, Adams. The scouts were there to see them, not me.

That didn't bother me. That I even merited a Pro Day was remarkable to some people. Plus, my teammates had earned the attention. Maybe at some point during the workout, the scouts would see me, too. I'd be lying if I didn't admit to using my underdog situation to feed the inner beast. The scene was familiar. The perception of long odds, lots of skeptics, the need to work harder than anyone else just to be noticed. The whole Nate-the-underdog catalog. I wasn't auditioning to be drafted higher. I was auditioning to get a shot.

Pro Day was like the Olympics. You got one or two chances to be the best you'd ever been. It was a day spent living on the edge. A slow time in my forty-yard dash might make the scouts look away. A lack of reps on the bench press might have them believing I wasn't strong enough. If I didn't jump sufficiently high or long, they might decide I lacked explosiveness. My measurables had to stand out. Something had to separate me from the other players in the workout.

"I'm gonna give you the tools to kill Pro Day," Lichter had said to all of us. "Take them or don't."

I was bred for this, starting with the backyard mini-Olympics at the house on High Street. My dad measured my height and weight. Then he'd have me do broad jumps and vertical jumps.

He'd see how many push-ups I could do in a minute, how many sit-ups in a minute. He'd clock how fast I could run a suicide sprint: five yards and back, ten and back, fifteen and back.

He wrote down the results. He wanted me to see my progress from year to year, to reinforce what our day-in, day-out workouts could achieve. In a very basic way, Pro Day wasn't much different from the mini-Olympics.

Each of those training sessions with Lichter would impact my audition. I brought the same mindset as always. I'd bust my ass so at the very least I would satisfy myself.

Some guys assumed that the adrenaline of the day would see them through. That's not real. Real is what you practice. It's the work you put in that allows you to perform on the biggest stage. Not some superpower that magically arrives exactly when you need it.

There was no pressure. To me, pressure is an expectation to do more than I've done before. I just needed to perform the way I was capable. I had no doubts. I wanted no What Ifs. When the moment came, I didn't need some superhuman performance. I just needed to meet my standard.

An agent told me, "You've got to wear yellow shoes. And a headband, so everyone will notice you."

I laughed at that. "I'm not putting on some circus show," I said. On my Pro Day, I wore black and gray.

It all came together in something called the L-drill. It's a standard test of agility and direction. I did it so well the scouts asked me to do it twice. They looked at their stopwatches, then looked at me, then looked at their stopwatches again. There must be a mistake.

An L-drill is symbolic of the nitpicky nature of an NFL Pro Day. It's not an especially relevant drill in determining potential pros. It's just one in the seemingly endless tests, physical and intellectual, teams use to try to make perfect an imperfect science. The lengths to which NFL teams go to identify good players can be crazy, and even with that, they miss on a lot of good football players. But when you're trying to impress men whose evaluations could change your life, you don't ask questions.

Six weeks earlier, Lichter said to me, "I want you to run the L-drill falling down drunk, because your foot placement and weight distribution is so good." For six weeks I worked on the finer points of an "inside leg turn." I pumped iron specifically in pursuit of more "explosion." A couple inches or one-tenth of a second can make a lifetime of difference. I worked every day to gain an inch.

For the L-drill, three cones are arranged in the shape of a sideways L. You start at the first cone, run straight ahead five yards to the second cone and back to the first, then run to the second cone and go 90 degrees to the right, then make a figure eight around the third cone and back around the second, before ending up back at the first cone. It sounds more complicated than it is.

A good time in the L-drill is 6.8 seconds. I did that first one in 6.25. It was the fastest L-drill time I'd ever known anyone to run. The scouts checked their watches and asked me to do it again. I did a 6.4.

I bench-pressed 225 pounds 23 times; I'd done 24 in workouts. A good score was 20 reps. No other defensive back did 23, not even at the combine.

I wanted a vertical jump of 36 inches. I did 39½.

A short-shuttle time of under 4 seconds is fast. I ran 3.91. That's super fast. I was at 4.3 seconds when I started training six weeks earlier. You see lots of guys fall when doing that drill because they're running too fast into the turns. Eric knew exactly how many steps I should take after each line touch to run the perfect drill. It was all about control.

After my vertical jump, the scouts started to watch me more closely. Then I killed that L-drill.

I can't tell you why in 2012 the New England Patriots drafted me in the sixth round, two months after my Pro Day. Maybe it was my Pro Day, maybe it was what I showed on film. It could have been Mike Vrabel, our defensive line coach my senior year, vouching for my character to Patriots coach Bill Belichick. Maybe it was all of that.

All I can tell you is that I had bedrock convictions to lean on. My foundation was unshakable. I had a job to do and a promise to keep. I'd prepared for this. I knew where I was going and how to get there. I didn't detour, I didn't give in to big moments. I saw my path clearly. And I killed my Pro Day.

FOURTEEN

Hiding in Plain Sight

My dad was focused and hardworking, but he had a playful side. He had his junkyard, his rugby, his son, and his girl. Everything else was strictly back seat. And he treated it that way. His cousin Brett Ebner called it "Jeff's Fuck It lifestyle." Away from work, if it wasn't fun, Jeff didn't do it.

A distinction should be noted: My dad was serious about rugby, but not in the way I was. He was dead set on smashes during games and parties after them. My devotion was limited to the pitch.

My dad had a frat-house sense of humor. As the best man at his friend Steve Finkel's wedding, he was in charge of all of Fink's stuff, including the clothes he'd wear at the altar. The day of the wedding, my dad wrote HELP in white shoe polish on the soles of Finkel's shoes. When Fink knelt at the altar, everybody in attendance started laughing.

My dad acted more on feel than convention. If something felt right, he was all in. Eating dessert first, skiing a back bowl in Aspen, buying a broken-down Mercedes at an auction then fixing it up. Things that wouldn't make sense to most people—changing clothes in the practice field parking lot—were second nature to him.

I didn't inherit that part of Jeff Ebner. I'm not impulsive. I think things through. There's much more hard-earned wisdom than Fuck It impulse with me, though I do have those impulses and draw on them when I need to. When it comes to decorum in public, I'm far more conventional than my dad was. I'm never going to shout "God bless America!" at a beautiful woman wearing an American-flag bikini walking by on the beach, as he once did.

My dad's Fuck It could be embarrassing. Sometimes I'd watch him and want to put my head in my hands. Unintentionally, he made me aware of how to act in public. I've always been reserved. You'd never describe Jeff Ebner that way.

His way wasn't for everyone, but anyone would be lucky to own his singular passion. Passion makes life interesting. And meaningful. Wanting to play professional football provoked that passion within me.

The NFL Draft was the culmination of it all. The passion, the purpose, the drive. The tank of self-belief that my dad always made sure was full.

I didn't expect to be drafted. I'd accomplished the three-year mission of getting myself noticed. I'd talked to coaches from a couple teams, the New England Patriots topping that list. I figured I'd be asked to some team's spring camp—"Organized team activities" in NFL parlance—and take my chances as an undrafted free agent. Not until Day 3 of the draft did I consider I might be picked. "Stay close to your phone," I was told by reps from a few teams.

I low-keyed the whole day. A player like me, on the fringes of the draft, has to keep his emotions on simmer. The last thing I wanted was to throw my own draft party and not be drafted.

In the morning, I worked out with Chelsey, my future wife. We spent the rest of the day in the basement of my mom's house in Dublin, Ohio, with a few friends and family. I'd gotten a call early in the day from the Patriots' special teams coach. By early afternoon, other teams were calling, doing last-minute mini-interviews. I was talking with someone from the Arizona Cardinals or St. Louis Rams when my agent called the house phone and told me to hang up. The Patriots were trying to reach me. Sure enough, the 508 area code popped up on the screen. "We're drafting you in the sixth round," Bill Belichick said.

When the call came from Foxboro, I was elated and I wanted to hug my dad. Effort always wins. That was Jeff Ebner's lesson, one of his gifts to me. My effort was the reason they called my name. With the 197th pick in the 2012 NFL draft . . .

The experts on ESPN were speechless. They came to the network set armed with mountains of inside info. They could tell you if Andrew Luck liked ketchup on his scrambled eggs and who the first two Robert Griffins were, before RG III. Their dossiers included nothing on me. Mel Kiper didn't have a brief-case full of tapes on Nate Ebner. When the Patriots picked me, ESPN went to a commercial.

There wasn't a compelling reason for them to know me. I played three downs of defense in three years in college. I went to Ohio State, sure, but my senior year was known more for tattoos than football.

I was a special teamer. NFL teams don't draft special team-ers, they find them: high draft picks who underperform; high picks the teams' personnel departments make mistakes on; over-achievers who know their best chance of getting paid to play football is to impress on special teams.

Why would anyone on ESPN have anything to say about me?

I chuckled. Man, this was typical Nate Ebner stuff. *No kegs on the sidelines here. You won't make the Buckeyes as a walk-on, and even if you do, you'll never play.*

Luke Fickell didn't think I'd be drafted, and he'd just been around me every day for eight months. Fick thought I'd get a look, nothing more. Being underestimated is a small part of my story, but it's a big small part. It has been in the script every page of the way. Why would this page be any different?

I've spent my life and career hidden in plain sight. I played rugby internationally while I was still in high school. Students knew the backup quarterback on the football team better. Nothing I've ever done would suggest I should be taken lightly, and yet . . .

I'm never sure how to react to this. I care and I don't. It bothers me, and it doesn't. I ignore it, and it motivates me. I hate that it motivates me—why should I give the doubters that credibility?—but I'm human. Dismissiveness, whether it's aimed at me personally or not, has always pissed me off.

On the one hand, it makes no difference what people who don't know me think of me. Giving their opinions a small space in my head detracts from my mission. On the other hand, being forever overlooked and underestimated is a form of disrespect. I can't help but take that personally.

Just because I never want to be seen as egotistical doesn't mean I don't have an ego.

People talking about things they don't know isn't unusual in a country where speech is free. It's a big reason I'm not talkative in public. I don't speak about things I don't know anything about because I've had people do that to me forever. And they're always wrong.

What's the quote? "Better to remain silent and be thought a fool than to speak and remove all doubt."

It does make my success, and the success of the teams I've played for, sweeter. When I think of how much the Patriots have been doubted in recent seasons—Tom Brady's getting old, the Belichick train is slowing—my individual issues don't amount to much. Except to me.

My dad could be the craziest player on the rugby pitch. He never disrespected an opponent by taking him lightly. That's how things go wrong. That's how you lose to an opponent who otherwise isn't worthy of defeating you.

I wasn't sitting in the basement of my mother's house in Dublin, Ohio, shaking my fist at the TV guys who didn't know me. I didn't even watch it. I was on the phone with the Patriots, making travel arrangements to be in Foxboro the next day.

I'd like to say everyone partied like it was New Year's and the ball was dropping in my mother's basement. They didn't. That's not me. Getting drafted was the first step toward the bigger goal. It validated what I'd been doing. It refocused me. I got the shot I wanted. Now I had to make it work.

In our workouts, my dad and I made a point of writing down every goal and noting every milestone along the way. The idea was always to reset the bar. We never reached a goal and stopped. We just kept reaching. What I do today doesn't guarantee my tomorrow. Striving is a lifetime job.

I flew to Foxboro the next day. I met Bill Belichick. "Are you ready to work?" he asked.

I assumed the question was rhetorical.

For a few minutes, I enjoyed being drafted, then I started to think about what was next. That's me. The joy never lingers. There's always something else to do. What I did yesterday isn't going to make my tomorrow.

The day after I left the 2016 Olympics in Rio de Janeiro, I was back on the practice field with the Patriots. I never assume success or take it for granted. It's just how I'm wired. There's always the next Next.

By the way, twelve years earlier, the Patriots had picked a quarterback in the sixth round, 199th overall, two spots behind me. He was a little-known QB from Michigan. His name was Tom.

FIFTEEN

Rookie Year

Being naturally obsessive is a friend and an enemy. As a little kid, I would spend all day drawing one bird, just so I'd draw him precisely the way I wanted. In elementary school, I laid out my next-day school clothes on the bottom of the bed. Before I went to sleep, I'd ask my mom to tell me five things I had to look forward to the next day. Then I'd tell her to close the door to my closet completely and leave the door to my room open at the same angle every night. That way, I'd know if anyone had been in my room while I was sleeping.

That's not normal.

But neither was my need to lift weights at age six, nor my insistence that I finish everything I started and finish it properly.

That obsession helped me achieve big things for more than a decade.

In my second regular-season game in the National Football League, I missed a block on punt protection. I was supposed to handle a six-foot-three, 250-pound Arizona Cardinals linebacker named Quentin Groves. I was six one, 210. He ran by me and blocked the punt near our goal line. The Cardinals took over at our 3 and scored three plays later. They beat us, 20–18. I thought I might get cut. Intellectually, I didn't believe the Patriots would let me go just two weeks after they had shown enough faith in me to keep me on the team. Emotionally, I wasn't so sure.

The NFL is a Darwinian place. *What have you done for me lately?* doesn't describe it. *What are you doing for me right now?* is closer to the truth. One day, there were one hundred players in camp. The next there were fifty-three. That's how it seemed. It occurred to me then that the Patriots could just get rid of me.

I'd experienced the dog-eat-dog at Ohio State. Every year, they brought in fresh players who wanted my job. That was nothing like this. The circle kept getting smaller. Staying on the inside required more and more of all I had. Darwin rode shotgun in my head. You could say I was obsessed with having a pro football career.

From the first day of camp, I felt like I could never catch my breath. I was in the clutches of this endlessly roaring machine and I was hyperventilating. Making it in the NFL meant everything to me. My making it meant nothing to the NFL.

The Pats' special teams coach, Scotty O'Brien, had a phrase

for it. "Ebner, you don't know what you don't know," he'd say. He applied that admonition to every situation, football or not. He wore it out, every day in training camp, to the point where its meaning to me became secondary to the irritation it provoked.

I hated hearing it five hundred times a day, and I didn't care if it was true. But it was true. O'Brien was right. I didn't know what I didn't know. I hadn't experienced football on its biggest stage. How could I possibly understand it? Maybe it was naivete. Maybe it was self-confidence. There isn't always an obvious line between the two. Whatever it was, it humbled me. Again.

I didn't intend just to pull on a preseason jersey and declare I'd made it. I wanted an actual career. A first contract, then another and another, until I could leave the game somewhat on my own terms. I'd be eligible after three seasons for an NFL pension. That would prove to me that I had, in fact, made it. But even a pension was only a starting point.

The reality was, it wasn't going to be that simple. If I didn't realize that on my own, Bill Belichick and his assistants clued me in.

My first meeting as a rookie, Bill tested the rookies' knowledge about Patriots veterans. And found it lacking. "This isn't college," Belichick said. "You don't get three nonconference warm-up games. This is the NFL. You haven't played a snap in this league. This is the first week of the season. It's a great time for you to shut up. You don't know what it's like. You couldn't possibly know."

That approach never changed. We always sucked. No matter

how well we played, or thought we were playing, it was never good enough. The philosophy started at the bottom, with the first-year grunts. Never praise a rookie. He needs to humble himself and realize he still has work to do, and that work will be endless.

If I made one good play, coaches would show me all the others I could have made better. Early that year, it confused me and pissed me off. It was the staff's way of reminding me that I didn't have it made. I knew that already. I didn't have it made. I'd known that my whole athletic career.

I took it personally. I'm busting my ass here. I didn't want to be talked to as if I wasn't.

It wasn't personal. I had to learn that. Bill wanted me to be as good as I could be. I was good on one play, or two; I could always be better. He wanted to optimize every little advantage. It was also a mind-mess, a way of keeping players (and assistant coaches) a little insecure about their jobs.

The whole point was to keep us from getting complacent. Just because we were better today than yesterday doesn't mean we shouldn't work to be even better tomorrow. Complacency leads to bad things. Not because you suddenly forget all you've learned, but because you're satisfied with it. Complacency doesn't work. No pun intended.

Even now, nearly a decade into my NFL career, I can have a good day, save a few hiccups, and I will focus on the hiccups. And I will say to myself, *Man, do I suck at football.*

External pressure didn't bother me a lot. I didn't need anyone pushing me. My pressure was self-imposed. As long as I satisfied myself with the work I put in, I could live with any result. All you can do is all you can do.

As the promise to my dad became more real, honoring it became more difficult. I started to press. The coaches were on my ass every day, the football terminology was harder than it was at Ohio State. I can grind with anyone, but this was six in the morning to nine at night, every day, in the football bunker. I couldn't escape.

MY OBSESSIVE PERSONALITY IS not leavened by Jeff Ebner's practiced sense of Fuck It. My personality influences everything I do. Or overdo, if I want to be truthful about it. I'm a perfectionist, if being perfect means I like to do things completely and correctly. My mom suggests I have OCD, but she laughs when she says it, so what does that mean?

I'll give you an example. My wife, Chelsey, and I have a cat. We bought the cat this beautiful drinking system. It looks like a fountain. It has a filter, among other things. Five or six pieces. Chelsey cleans it by rinsing out the bowl. Really?

I take the whole thing apart. I scrub each piece. It takes about ten minutes. Because what's the point in having a clean bowl when the rest of the fountain is dirty? Good enough is never good enough.

I never wanted anything more than an NFL career. I wasn't obsessive about it. I was beyond obsessive. This was about the last promise I'd ever made to the most important person in my life. I couldn't screw this up.

Within reason, anything is possible if you're willing to sacrifice everything. Right? I was at the point of sacrificing everything, just as I'd done as a Buckeye. The difference was, for the first time in my life, I didn't know how it would turn out. I couldn't just impose my will on the situation, overwhelm it with work ethic, and have complete confidence I'd succeed.

I never doubted my abilities. I could hang with these guys. I did question how much I wanted to do this. There is no leaving the daily grind of an NFL season. July to January is a seven-month stay in the football motel. In New England, maybe even more so. The way you deal with that defines to an extent who you are and what you want.

It got deeply into my head. I needed more of my dad's Fuck It attitude. I thought I had to be perfect. And that was before I allowed the blocked punt.

I wasn't just a special teamer. I was getting reps at safety, more than I ever did at Ohio State. As a rookie trying to make the team, I did everything I could to make myself useful.

My personal life suffered. I was a zombie to Chelsey, then my girlfriend. She remembers 2012 like it was last night's nightmare: "You had no personality. You were a robot, always tired. I wanted to do things. You wouldn't get off the couch."

I wasn't lazy. I was spent, every which way.

"When you got to the NFL, I took a back seat. Your heart

and soul went to your team," was Chelsey's accurate diagnosis. "You didn't have anything left." Chelsey sacrificed starting her career in medical sales to be there for me. She felt unappreciated and moved home for a while. "I wasn't going to stay home, eat brie, and take a lot of selfies," she said. "I needed to be on my own a little."

Chelsey was not someone who needed me to help define her. She didn't love having "NFL player's girlfriend" attached to her identity. I respected that. Chelsey aspired to her own career. Being "Mrs. Nate Ebner" didn't appeal to her. Even today, she doesn't tell people who her husband is until they get to know her. She says when people discover we're married, they sometimes assume she lacks ambition. "People think it's weird I work," she said not long ago.

I love her independence and respect her ambition. We both have working moms, so the concept isn't exactly unfamiliar.

Plus, I'm never going to be the easiest man to live with. When we were dating, she said I was "hard to read and shy." I didn't give her a lot to work with. "Mysterious," was Chelsey's take. "I never knew if you liked me."

The truth was, I liked her a lot. I was busy, though (imagine that), playing rugby and spring football at Ohio State, while she was at Ohio University, a couple hours east.

We formed our initial bond in the gym. She ran track in high school and did some modeling. At OU, she worked as a fitness manager. Chelsey knew her way around a gym. I didn't have to cut my workouts short for her when we worked out together. She even made a pilgrimage to my mom's house in suburban Columbus, where I still used some of my dad's old metal.

"I struggled," Chelsey remembers. "It wasn't really functional."

To her credit, she rolled with Jeff Ebner's simple heavy metal. Personally, I didn't care what she or anyone else thought about my dad's weights. They were fine. "It's not like going to LA Fitness," I said.

The relationship grew, obviously. We got married in April 2019.

MY ROOKIE-YEAR ISSUES subsided eventually. I adjusted to the NFL life. Chelsey did, too. That rookie year was rough though.

Even before training camp started, I knew I'd need to learn the language of Patriots football. Literally. The verbiage they used to describe things in the defensive and special teams meeting rooms was unique. The Patriots had their own language. It was sort of a parallel English.

I made two hundred flash cards to deal with that. Each card had the Patriots' jargon on one side and what it meant on the other. All summer before camp started, I studied those cards like they were the Bible, because in some very tangible way, they were. If the Pats cut me, it would not be because I was too lazy to learn the language.

If they decided I wasn't big/fast/strong enough, OK. The NFL is full of physical freaks. I can't control that. Knowing the playbook was something I could control.

As it turned out, I was in for every special teams play that preseason. I even played some safety and intercepted a couple passes. I still didn't know what I didn't know, but I knew enough to survive. That's what training camp was all about that first summer. Surviving.

I didn't feel any huge joy when I made the team. I was too tired to feel anything but relief. I'm not one to celebrate my own success, anyway. I take a minute to catch a little satisfaction. Then I start thinking about what I have to do to stay on the team I just made. I wasn't there just to live in the moment. I wanted lots of moments. A long career-ful.

After the blocked punt, I spent a lot of time looking over my shoulders and asking them to bear the weight of the world. I'd never had a bad play like that at Ohio State, so I had no experience to lean on. And I internalized everything.

I needed my dad there. "Shit happens," he'd have said. "Learn from it. Pick yourself up and do better next time."

Unless you're Tom Brady, life as a pro football player is a sort of measured desperation. I never felt safe. I still don't. That's by design. As I said, coaches want their players to be insecure. It's easier to control us that way. It's leverage. They also want us supremely confident in ourselves. It's a strange contradiction. The longer you play, the worse it gets. The more money you make, the better player you need to be. The minute you can be replaced by someone better and cheaper, you're gone. It's a precarious way to make a living.

I believed that getting released would be the end of the world. The league didn't put that on me. The coaches didn't. I put it on myself. I had to stop worrying and start overcoming. Control what I could control, clear my mind. Overcome the physical and mental exhaustion and get off the damned couch, literally and figuratively.

A quick word about playing safety:

It has been the singular frustration of my NFL career.

When the Pats gave me a chance my rookie year, I wasn't ready for it. When I'd gained enough experience to feel comfortable with it, they didn't play me. I needed a chance to blossom. I've never gotten it.

I think I'm honest about my abilities and limitations. Just because someone is confident doesn't also make them blind. I could play safety. I've seen my competition over the years. I know I'm capable.

I didn't get the looks at safety in my second and third years as a Patriot that I got my rookie year. After a while, players can get labeled. As my special teams fortunes improved, my safety time declined.

I see guys with better "measurables"—height, weight, forty-yard times, reps on the bench press—who can't play football as well as I can. They're physical specimens, but they can't (or won't) tackle. Sometimes, players who have always relied on their speed don't understand the game. They can run, but they don't study.

This stuff drives me crazy. I try not to think about it, because I can't control it, and the negativity wastes energy. And really, with all that said, I am grateful to have played for a coach who valued special teams and appreciated my contribution enough to have kept me around almost a decade.

I prepared to play safety as a rookie. That's what the flash cards were for. Meantime, I fretted over my mistakes as a special teamer.

As it happened, I did have someone to lean on besides Chelsey, whose patience with my brooding was saintly: my dad's cousin Brett Ebner. Brett was twelve years younger than Jeff. They were always close, which guaranteed my dad had a big influence on Brett's coming of age. Nothing says "growing up fast" more than a grown man taking a teenager barhopping.

"I'm thirteen, he's twenty-five," Brett recalled. "We're drinking and picking up girls."

At some point, Brett's family moved to California, but Brett would come back to Ohio in the summer for a month at a time, and hang out with my dad. They were alike in a lot of ways. Intense, but always ready to have fun. I inherited the first half of that equation.

My dad didn't like to talk on the phone—too much small talk—but he loved talking to Brett. Brett would be on his way to work in Los Angeles and use the stuck-in-traffic commute to call my dad. The way Brett describes it, if they talked for thirty-five minutes, thirty of them were about me.

"What's new?" Brett would ask.

That was my dad's entry to talk briefly about my stepmother ("Ames is good"), my grandfather ("the old man is good"), and about the business (also good), before he'd launch into a monologue about my latest workout successes. "All Nate's workout numbers," Brett recalled. "Benching, squatting, rowing. It was like I was a scout. I mean, Nate was fifteen."

"Hollywood," my dad would tell Brett, "Nate's gonna be a pro athlete."

After my dad died, Brett took it upon himself to become more involved in my life. He never expected anything for it. He came back for the funeral and my mom asked him to talk to me. "You're one of the closest people to Jeff he has left." Brett saw me in the depths of my hoodie-shrouded, video-game funk.

He'd fly in for my games, at Ohio State and with the Patriots, buy a ticket and put himself up, hoping to see me afterward, but not insistent about it. "I knew I was not going to replace Jeff," Brett explained, years later. "But I knew Jeff well, and Nate in some respects is a lot like his father. The passion, the confidence. I could speak to him in a way he could respect and trust."

It was a comfort to me that Brett was close enough to my dad; he knew what I needed, which was simply someone to listen. He was very present, same as Jeff Ebner. I talked to Chelsey and my mom, too, but Brett understood what I was saying. He was my voice of reason, he reaffirmed what I was thinking.

Brett didn't want anything from the relationship but the relationship. His support was genuine, and after I allowed that blocked punt, I needed all the support I could get.

We talked about not letting that play kill my confidence. We agreed I was at my best when I wasn't stressing or obsessing about something. Football is an emotional game, but if you play it with too much emotion, you waste energy and don't think clearly. I had to pick my spots. I loved the puppy, but I was squeezing him too hard.

I enjoyed Brett's company, partly for that connection he had with my dad. I wouldn't try to avoid Brett. Most of the rest of the world, I'd try to avoid.

Negative people, whiners, and people who feel sorry for themselves mess with my chi. If something's not productive, I'm not wasting time on it. Brett was positive. A month after I'd allowed the block, Brett found a photo of me online, standing in the stadium tunnel before a night game, bathed in light. Brett wrote, "You're never alone. He's always with you," a heartfelt reference to my dad. I kept that on my phone for a long time.

I think Brett's friendship with me has helped him, too. He saw Jeff in me. He even called me Jeff once, on the phone a few years ago. He understood my dad. He was a lot like him. They shared that Fuck It bond. Brett still hears regularly from my stepmom, Amy, and saw firsthand how she took a back seat sometimes to my relationship with my father.

Brett feels some of my pain. After the Patriots beat the Seahawks in Super Bowl XLIX, our family met in a small restaurant near Phoenix to celebrate. Brett started thinking about how much my dad would have enjoyed the moment. He had to go outside and compose himself.

We talked a lot that year, and it all helped. I was buried so deeply in my own tunnel, it didn't occur to me that my experiences weren't that different from every rookie in the league, and just about every veteran.

THE PRESSURE FOR most players is in knowing their window is so small. They have to produce or they risk getting labeled as a guy who can't get it done. The machine waits for no one. Your game is picked apart and your flaws are highlighted. New guys are coming in all the time. If you don't get on top of it, you find yourself on the street before you have time to ask why. And every year is a new year. You can't get comfortable, and that's true if you're a rookie or a ten-year vet. No coach cares what you did last year if you can't do it this year.

I grew a little from the mistake against Arizona. I started studying the guys I'd be blocking in games. If the guy was big like Quentin Groves, I wasn't going to wrestle him. I'd cut him. Go low at his legs, make him try to jump over me. For me it was the best way to handle bigger rushers. Take their legs out.

Patriots special teams coach Scotty O. didn't teach his players to cut. Looking back on it, I was proud I had some success doing it Scotty's way. Now, I'm gonna cut a big-ass dude, every time.

A month after the blocked punt, we played the Seattle Seahawks, in Seattle. I had a situation similar to what I faced against Groves. Big guy, trying to run me over. I got low and flipped him. Maybe I still didn't know what I didn't know. But I knew then I could play in the league.

I was able to lighten up on myself a little after that. I realized what I'd known all along, yet buried: I could live with not making the New England Patriots; I couldn't have tried any harder than I had. "NFL football player" is one of the most competitive jobs on the planet. One percent of the top 1 percent. If it doesn't work out, fuck it. Move on. There's no shame in that. I always had rugby, even if it meant playing overseas.

That was the story of my rookie year. Not the rituals imposed on rookies at training camp or the specific demands made of me, mentally and physically. The act of indulging the promise, losing my grip on it for the first time, then rallying. That was the lesson.

I always felt my dad's presence. His death didn't lessen his influence on me. If anything, his death made his sway sharper.

I played for the perfect head coach for me. Bill Belichick was a guy who valued intangibles and recognized winning players. I played on the best team in football. I'd looked at doubt for the first time, and I didn't flinch. My only job was to keep things rolling. Rookie year was OK. And then it was gone.

SIXTEEN

Finding My Niche

By my second year, I understood the drill in New England. I didn't have it made (no one does there), but I did have an idea of how to stay employed. There's a lot to say about the so-called Patriot Way, in terms of the success it has produced, but it's not complicated: Work hard, do your job, put the team first, and come to work each day with the idea of getting better.

It fit me, but I was no perfect Patriot. There have been lots of perfect Patriots since Bill Belichick started coaching the team in 2000, players who lived Bill's ethos. But in some significant ways, I could not have found a better team to play for.

I want to earn what I get. Bill's all about that. You don't build the dynasty the Pats have without finding like-minded people who see what you see and want what you want. Bill's obsessive. I'm obsessive. He'll take chances on guys like me.

In one sense, I don't know him well. I don't know a player who does. Bill keeps his emotional distance, so closeness doesn't impair his judgment when moves need to be made. In another sense, I know Bill like the man in the mirror. We admire and respect the same things. We hold ourselves to high standards. We don't have time for those who don't feel the same.

No one is made to feel comfortable with the Patriots. You might do lots of things right on Sunday, but coaches on Monday will find what you did wrong and emphasize it. That serves a couple ends:

It makes you understand that you're never as good as you could be (or you think you are), and it breeds an insecurity that drives you. If you think you're all that in New England, you won't be a Patriot very long.

It took me my rookie year to understand that. My dad wasn't that way with me. At all. He was nothing but positive. It was important to him that I felt good about what I was doing. Jeff Ebner was can-do all the time, an approach that gave me self-confidence and total belief that if I worked hard enough, no goal was out of reach. Jim Tressel preached the same sermon.

That wasn't how things worked in New England. Your self-esteem was not their concern. I learned not to worry about the constant criticism. You can't walk on eggshells and play football. You can't be scared of screwing up. You have to play with almost an unconscious mind. Let it fly, obey the dog within. You can't be so afraid to mess up that you mess up.

Bill sets the standard for coaches, too. Don't be satisfied, get the most from your players, respect them as people and they'll return the respect.

You can't take it personally. Bill's not trying to make you fearful. He just wants you to do your job. When you do, and when it's helpful to the team as a whole, he'll point that out, too. He's not hard to get along with. Just be accountable for your mistakes and fix them.

So I dug in.

You wouldn't think playing special teams could require a detailed, analytical mind. As anyone who plays teams will tell you, covering kickoffs demands that you be instinctive, not intellectual. Kickoffs are nothing but a bunch of individual fights. Line up, run as fast as you can and go to the guy with the ball.

No one in his thinking mind would recommend full-speed collisions with another human being as a good way to support your family. Body as projectile? On game days, you have to be a little off.

Punts are different, especially with the job I have. Since my second season I have been the Patriots PP—personal protector— the player who lines up between the long snapper and the punter. The position can be as mental as nearly any in football. The PP is the QB of the punt team. He calls the protections, based on the rush he sees. If he doesn't put people in the right spots, the punt team is chaos. Not only does he have to react to what he's seeing, he has to predict what he'll see next, before and after the ball is snapped.

If a team gives us an all-out rush look, the personal protector has to protect against it. If a team drops rushers out to help cover our gunners, showing a return look, before the ball is snapped, the PP could change the call from protecting against a punt rush to getting guys out in coverage against a return. That's when a PP's instant analysis and correct call can be crucial.

That has nothing to do with running like a crazed dog for fifty yards or blowing up a return man. It's about checks and audibles, seeing what the other team is trying to do, then exploiting it. As the PP, I have seen so many rushes, watched so much film, I can usually predict what the rush is going to be.

I learned at Ohio State that I wasn't getting my NFL shot as a safety. When I made it to the league, I knew I had to make myself necessary, even as I competed for a spot in the secondary.

It's like Tabasco sauce. The McIlhenny family of Avery Island, Louisiana, has produced Tabasco since 1868. It still uses the same ingredients—tabasco peppers, vinegar, salt—in the same proportions. The recipe doesn't change, and neither does the diligence. The essence of playing special teams doesn't revolutionize every decade, the way offenses do. It's all a matter of doing it consistently well. *Consistency* is just about the best word in the English language.

During my time with the Patriots, I watched and analyzed. I saw Tom Brady, admittedly not an elite athlete, win six rings by being a step ahead of everyone else. I watched Matthew Slater make seven Pro Bowls as a special teams player, by using his head as much as his body. I saw all kinds of solid veterans come through our locker room and embrace the way Bill Belichick runs things. I saw a few vets who didn't embrace his way leave the building before their times.

It's like what Jeff Ebner said: Adjust. Modify. Adapt.

It's funny. When I was eight years old and performing the mini-Olympics in the backyard, I didn't wonder why my dad was writing all my statistics in a little black book. I paid attention to what he was saying because he was my dad and I loved him more than anyone. As time went on, I applied the Olympic record-keeping to reps and sets on the weight machines and extended that to my times on the rowing machine. I did this for several years, never really pondering the point of writing everything down. And then at some, unknowable moment, it became part of me. No less real than an arm or a leg.

I came to realize what my dad was trying to show me. *Look at how much better you did on the long jump this year, Nate! It's because of how hard you worked all year long.* Along the road to understanding the beauty of hard work and accountability, I became analytical and detail oriented. I grasped the impact that precision can have on performance. How can I do this squat more efficiently so I don't hurt myself? How do I execute this ninety-degree turn more precisely in the L-drill to make the NFL scouts stare in disbelief at their stopwatches?

How does a personal protector call the right protection so his team doesn't lose a game on a blocked punt? On a play that lasts fewer than three seconds, speed and precision are everything. A punt return is controlled chaos, but without the control it's just chaos.

I'm analytical about everything. I can't go to a movie just to be entertained. I need to analyze it. Why did the director shoot that scene that way? What else are they telling about the story and the characters through the dialogue? What is the music trying to make me feel at any particular moment? What themes are they trying to highlight throughout the movie? I'm not gonna invest two hours and not have something to say about it. You can like a movie or not. Just be able to tell me why.

If I'm doing squats and my knees hurt, I'll watch someone who's doing the same exercise on painless knees. Why do mine hurt? What can I do to ease the pain? It could be my posture. It could be my form. It could be anything. I watch others and analyze. Sometimes, I'll see a detail that makes a difference.

Some people read books for content. The story is enough. Others read them for style. The words mean more than the story. I'm a mix of both, because one without the other is only half as good as it could be.

My dad would see people do things he couldn't do—or at least had never tried—and ask why he couldn't do what they were doing. *I can fix this engine. I have the manual, I can read. If that guy can do it, why can't I?* He applied that logic to everything in his life and, by extension, to mine.

Nate, of course you can play rugby against men twice your age when you're thirteen years old. Of course you can be the best player

*on our Scioto Valley club team just three years later. You and I can
ski the back bowls of Aspen, Colorado, as complete novices. Look at
those people. They're older than we are. They can't be in as good
shape. They're doing it. Why can't we?*

This was my dad's version of analysis. Typically blunt, occasionally naive. We no more could ski Aspen's back bowls than
slalom down High Street in Springfield. But I've packed that sort
of thinking with me ever since. Why can't I be the best personal
protector in the NFL?

I got good enough at it, I could be a pain in the ass in meetings. I asked lots of questions. It's never enough for me just to see
something work properly. I want to know why. There is no "that's
the way it is" with me. Bullshit. If you're going to ask me to take
responsibility—for myself, for my teammates, for the outcome of
a play—I need to hear you say more than "that's how we do it
here."

I never understood how players could fall asleep in meetings.
If your head isn't ready for Sunday, the rest of you is going to
be compromised. Some guys sit in meetings and nod. They do
what they're told, the best they can. I need to know the why. If I
don't see the reasoning behind something, I'm going to create a
problem.

I have to make the play work. I can't be compromised by the
game plan. When the other team runs a certain punt rush, I'm
the one calling the protection. When we looked at the film Monday, Bill was talking to me, not the special teams coach.

Coaches aren't there when the bullets are flying. They can

overanalyze it. They can watch so much special teams film, they start seeing ghosts. They'll look for stuff that isn't there. Players can, too, but the good ones let their informed instincts take over. They succeed because they play fast and can react to what they're seeing as it happens. Coaches can overprepare without knowing what it's like in real time. I've had coaches tell me as the PP to chip one rusher, then block another. That's crazy. This stuff happens at a million miles an hour. Don't burden guys with having to think in real time when their jobs depend on reacting.

We call the weak link on the opponent's punt team "the fish." If there's a clear fish, and I look at our game plan and it doesn't attack the fish, I want a reason. *Why aren't we going after him? We sat here and watched all this film. We saw who the fish was, and we're not going after him?*

I don't mean to be confrontational. But I need to understand. After I've watched all of an opponent's punts from the previous five years, I can't sit there and say, OK, I'll just run what we call.

Ryan Allen was the Patriots' punter for six years and has come to be one of my closest friends. Ryan came up the way I did. He didn't start punting until his junior year in high school. He walked on at Oregon State, then finished at Louisiana Tech. He signed with the Pats in 2013 as an undrafted free agent and earned three Super Bowl rings until the team cut him in August 2019. He's still working, with the Atlanta Falcons.

We are totally different people. He's outgoing; I'd rather not be. He's in the center of the party; I'm holding up a wall, if I go at all. Ryan appreciates life's finer things; I'm good with sweats.

For my weeklong bachelor party, it was Ryan who convinced me that spending $25,000 to rent a nice chalet for a week in Whistler, British Columbia, was OK. We do have a few big things in common: He takes accountability for himself, he's grateful for what the NFL has given him, and he knows when silence is golden.

Ryan got past my resting bitch face to see I was a good teammate and pretty good at my job. Now, we're movie buddies and snowboarding freaks. Ryan said this about me recently:

"Nate looks into each situation and sees beyond the obvious. He knows it's all about efficiency, because everything happens so fast. His knowledge alone is worth a couple million a year. What he gives you in the classroom makes it easier for everyone to understand. At the end of my tenure with the Patriots, he was damned near running the (special teams) meetings."

It helps that I've been a personal protector longer than almost anyone in the league. After eight or nine seasons with the Patriots, I should have known our protection schemes as well as anyone.

The best personal protectors know the job well enough that no matter the situation, they can work it to their team's advantage. Matt Slater said I understand the kicking game better than anyone he's been around. "In the middle of a play, I've heard him call out the return. He identifies on the fly how they're blocking us, because we've seen it on film all week," Slater said.

He was also my best friend on the team. Matthew and I were in on every special teams play together, in the same meetings day after week after year. He's one of the highest-character people I've ever met. He also has little patience for people who aren't. We designate them as "frauds."

Slate's good at spotting frauds, but not as good as I am. He's more empathetic on the subject. He cuts guys some slack. I'm adamant. By my definition, frauds are people with inconsistent character traits. What's the saying? "If you don't stand for something, you'll fall for anything." We both want people to be who they are, all the time. To stand for the same things. You can't have a locker room full of players who are about the team one day and about themselves the next.

I think Slate has always seen that in me. I'm consistent in my work habits and my respect for people who put the team first. I've never tried to be someone else. I shoot straight. I don't think my attitude is a big reason I'm still around the league. I'm sure of it.

I made second team All-Pro in 2016, when I led the NFL in special teams tackles. The Patriots haven't had a punt blocked since 2015. Special teams have blocked seven opponents' punts since then. Teams had significant impacts on each of the three Super Bowl wins I was involved in.

Bill Belichick has an affection for special teams few head coaches share. He appreciates how special teams can win games, either directly with points or subtly, by influencing field position. Bill's obsessiveness doesn't allow for slighting special teams.

I also believe that Bill values the team-first strivers that populate his special teams. Nothing gets him going like watching selfish football. Personal fouls after a play, defensive ends running up the field looking for a sack in an obvious running situation. A running back not taking care of the ball after he has just made a first down.

The Patriots are in tune with situational football, prepared for the moment. No moment is too big, no situation too small. Some teams let the small things slip. The Pats don't. The difference between most NFL teams is minimal. Every advantage is magnified. The Patriots study more, they condition more. They try to know their opponents a little better than their opponents know them.

One week during the 2018 season, we were preparing to play the Chicago Bears. That week, Bill did the usual, telling us everything we needed to know about every single player we'd be seeing on Sunday. He took it a step further, so now I know the entire history of the Bears organization, from their ownership to George Halas to how they started in the league.

Bill's a football historian. We watched all this stuff about the original Soldier Field and how it hosted the first game between Notre Dame and Southern Cal. Did you know that game drew 130,000 people? The previous week, we'd played the Kansas City Chiefs, coached by Andy Reid. Reid is one of the godfathers of the West Coast offense, so we got a history lesson about the West Coast offense.

The Patriots culture is instilled by Bill and driven home by everyone in the locker room. Tom Brady was in the middle of that photo. He leads by example. He doesn't take days off. Why should I? The biggest winner in the history of the NFL was also the first player at the facility, most days. The amazing thing about Tom is not the results he has gotten, but the work he has put in to get those results.

Bill owns his share of accountability, too. We had bad games when he said, "We stunk. The reason? You're looking at him. Good players can't overcome bad coaching."

I'd never worked for another team until I signed with the Giants in March 2020, so I can't say New England's way is the best. I can only say the Patriots are constantly looking for an edge, in a league where even the smallest edge matters.

I had run the NFL's Darwinian gauntlet and found my niche. The Patriot Way: Work hard, do your job, try to get better at it every day. I always got that message. I was all but born with it.

We can go through life accepting what happens to us. Or we can take charge and have a say. Concepts such as "fate" and "coincidence" aren't for me. Life isn't a palm reading. I didn't have a say in losing my dad when I was nineteen years old. But I had a chance to impact everything that followed in a way befitting his legacy.

SEVENTEEN

Glory

E very NFL team goes into a season wanting to win the Super Bowl, even if its odds aren't great. Wanting and doing are two different things.

I wanted to play well for the Patriots, for my teammates, my coaches, and myself. I wanted to help us maintain the standard set in New England since February 2002, when the Patriots won the first of six Super Bowls. Saying you want something is never enough. It's the starting line, but it's just words. You find out how serious you are about it when you start grinding for it every day. When you get to Week 9 of the season and you still have half the year left just to qualify for the playoffs, how much do you still want that Super Bowl trophy?

Are you getting to work before the sun rises, and leaving well after it sets? What are you doing when no one is watching and the season feels endless?

The Patriots don't want. They do. Every day, every personnel move, every thought is conceived with the intention of winning a championship. As soon as you win this one, you start planning to win the next.

I have three Super Bowl rings. They stay locked up. I wear them very occasionally, usually for public appearances. I'm not a jewelry guy. You will not see me wearing a $30,000 necklace with my uniform number outlined in diamonds. Or a $500 T-shirt. That stuff is look-at-me silly. If you need material things, that suggests you require validation from other people.

The last thing I'm about is flashing a look-at-me ring that weighs more than a bag of groceries. I love them, though. I love the rings. They represent the mountaintop and the climb required. The everyday NFL grind must be endured to be appreciated. (Or cursed.) Not many people can do it, not for years and years, and definitely not with the New England Patriots, who are a different breed of beast.

All the guys that have been Patriots as long or longer than I was are tough dudes. I look at them and I know what they've been through. What I'd been through. Some people can call on their inner beasts for big tasks. They own the mental sand that says, *Nothing is going to break me.* That's the test in New England. As Jeff Ebner put it, "Conquer the pain and the glory will last forever."

The rings tangibly confirm who I believe myself to be.

Each was earned in a different way. Three wins, three ways of winning. Each provoked different feelings. The first one—Super Bowl XLIX, February 1, 2015, against Seattle—was my third year in the league. I carved a few minutes for myself two hours before the game, warming up without pads on the field. I looked up at the stands filling and the cameras everywhere. The lights were still dim, but the buzz of energy was building. And I thought this: *Holy shit, I'm playing in the Super Bowl.*

Playing in the Super Bowl was never part of the dream. Playing in the NFL was.

I reserved some head space for my dad. It's always the same: Before the game, I'm wishing he were there. When I'm playing, I'm imagining him there and he's not and I can't do anything about it. It's the same circle of emotions. It's a thought that never goes anywhere. Same as one thousand times before.

Only this time, it was a little different. Six years earlier, almost to the day, I was prepping for the walk-on workout at Ohio State, wondering if I'd have a college career and what that might lead to. And now I'm in the Super Bowl. What are the chances?

I wonder: Was honoring my promise to my dad the little extra I've needed to push through? To get to that moment, alone, on the field at the University of Phoenix Stadium in Glendale, Arizona? Maybe. Probably. When I tired of the grind and needed a little more strength, I found it through the promise.

We beat the Seahawks, 28–24. We came back twice from fourteen points down. Nearly everyone will remember Malcolm

Butler's interception of a Russell Wilson pass in the end zone with twenty-six seconds to play. As the personal protector, I remember the two punts we could have had blocked. On one of them, I had to block two guys coming right up the middle. Chip one, get in the way of the other. That's not sound protection. The Seahawks should have blocked that one. It would have changed the game. They missed it.

After the game, I met my family and friends for the Super Bowl after-party. The joy was raucous and everywhere, but we found a corner to celebrate a little more quietly. I'm not Rob Gronkowski. There were no private jets to Miami for me, no visits to the clubs along South Beach. Just a nice dinner with people I loved. My celebration was in the journey I'd made. How far I'd come, how many doubters I'd silenced. That was enough.

The ring ceremony was in June. I enjoyed that as much as anything. It's classy and genuine. No one is there except the people who earned the right to attend.

It's laid-back, at Mr. Kraft's house in suburban Boston. Robert Kraft has owned the team since 1994. The Patriots' success owes as much to his ownership as to anyone. The Lombardi Trophies are all there, in a row. Six of them, at last count.

United States Marines in full dress brought out the rings, in wood-grained boxes, literally on a silver platter. A marine in white gloves handed me my box.

I've never needed a ring to see my dream as fulfilled. A ring is gravy. But man, what a feeling. Opening that box and holding that championship ring with your name on it. What sweet validation of the work you've put in. It's the ultimate expression of teamwork.

Two years later, we beat the Atlanta Falcons in overtime, 38–31, in Super Bowl LI. We were down 28–3 at halftime and none of us had any doubt we would win. Bill said, "We can't score twenty-eight points on one play. One play at a time. We'll score, stop them, and score again."

That's what we did. We finally caught the Falcons with fifty-seven seconds left in regulation time, on a touchdown pass and a two-point conversion to tie things at 28. We won in overtime. When you're down 28–3, every inch counts. Everyone had to play almost perfectly after halftime. It was the greatest example of a so-called total team effort I can recall.

It was also a textbook tribute to the importance of special teams. Super Bowl LI will be remembered as the greatest comeback in Super Bowl history. What will be forgotten—what *has* been forgotten, even by the few who noticed at all—was that the Falcons started six of their ten possessions inside their 20-yard line. And there was this:

The Falcons led 28–20 with the ball and 5:53 left. Because of our very good kickoff coverage, they started that possession at their 10-yard line. Any sort of score likely would have clinched the win for them. They drove to our 23-yard line where, on second-and-eleven, Trey Flowers sacked Matt Ryan for a twelve-yard loss. Officials flagged Atlanta for holding on the next play, and the Falcons had to punt.

Great defense? Absolutely. Does anyone even entertain the notion that circumstances could have been much different had our kickoff coverage team not pinned Atlanta back to its ten? "Hidden yards" they're called.

I led the NFL in special teams tackles that year. I was second-team All-Pro. I enjoyed another ring ceremony. I represented the team at the ESPYs. But 2016 was about way more than football.

EIGHTEEN

The Heart Wants What the Heart Wants

I was part of the best football team in the world, working in the most popular sport in the country, enjoying all of it in the prime of my career. Life was very, very good.

And yet, I dreamed of doing something else. Not permanently. Just for the summer. A how-I-spent-my-summer-vacation challenge. My laser focus zeroed in on a sport I hadn't played competitively since college. That amounted to a six-year layoff by the summer of 2016.

Sometimes, we do things for love. Nothing is more motivating or crazy or holds more chances for glory or disaster than something done for love.

I wanted a chance to play rugby Sevens in the 2016 Summer Olympics in Rio. I wanted it with the same white-hot obsession that consumed me as a walk-on at Ohio State and as a newly minted member of the New England Patriots. The only difference was, this desire was even more implausible.

I was completely willing to jeopardize a lucrative football career to do it. If anything, that gave extra authenticity to the quest.

I would play out my rookie contract in the 2015 season, sign an extension with the Patriots, and ask them for their OK to let me make a run at the Olympics. If they said, *Yes, good luck, we'll be here waiting with a new contract in August after the rugby competition ends*, then perfect. If they said no, I'd thank them for four great seasons and take my chances in the free agent market after the Olympics. Either way, I was going to do this.

It was no spur-of-the-moment call. It wasn't serendipitous. I don't do serendipity. It was a thought-out plan that actually hatched in 2009, when the International Olympic Committee announced that rugby would return to the 2016 Games, after a ninety-two-year absence. It'd be Sevens rugby, for a couple reasons: Sevens matches last just fourteen minutes, so you could play three matches in a day and the rugby competition would fit into a two-day Olympic window. Also, Sevens was seen as having a broader international appeal (read: US television appeal) than Fifteens, because of its speed and relentless action. Seven-minute halves work well with limited attention spans.

In 2009, I was playing football at Ohio State. I had no idea what I'd be doing seven years down the road. Hopefully, playing in the NFL. But to actually consider that room for Olympic rugby could be found within my growing NFL career? That was fantasy stuff. It occupied no space in my head in 2009. All I knew then was that someday I'd get back on the pitch.

In 2014, the US side qualified for the Rio Games. That made my dream tangible. I always knew I'd get back in the sport. But come on. For an Olympic shot?

In December 2015, Pat Clifton, a writer for the online magazine *Rugby Today*, wrote about my quest to play rugby in the Olympics. Clifton explained the tight window I would have to get in rugby shape before the Olympic tryouts in June. He wrote about my looming status as a free agent. I could leave the Pats, make the rugby run, then take my chances on the NFL's open market after the Olympics, assuming I made the US side.

Clifton noted that, according to US Sevens coach, Mike Friday, getting in Sevens shape takes about eight weeks. The time I'd need would be somewhat less, given I was already a pro athlete.

That article gave the dream much-needed reality. It wasn't impossible. In fact, it was doable.

For a few years, I'd been talking to people within the game. I'd stayed connected generally over the previous six years with everyone from my dad's rugby buddies to the Scioto Valley club and national coaches. Now, I wanted to know the lay of the Olympic land. The players, the coaches, the system. Where did I fit? How might the team receive me?

I'm not an eighteen-year-old high school senior, running around Wales while my classmates are reading *Huckleberry Finn*. I'm a businessman in a career for short-timers.

I had several lunches in Boston with Alex Magleby, the director of player performance for USA Rugby and the national Sevens team coach in 2012 and 2013. What would my path look like? I spent time with Al Caravelli at his home in Connecticut, to eat dinner and watch rugby film. I asked him, "How realistic are my chances of making the team?" Caravelli was a former national Sevens coach. Magleby followed him for two years. Mike Friday was the current coach.

Caravelli believed my chances were good. He explained later, "I knew if Nate had three months to get ready, he'd make the Olympic team. I went all-out to make sure he got a chance."

Caravelli put in a good word for me with Nigel Melville, the CEO of USA Rugby. "Just give Nate a look," Al said.

Anthony Schlegel and I hashed it out in the football off-season, while working out in the OSU baseball weight room/dungeon. "If you tried out and didn't make it, or if you did, and you never played another down in the NFL, could you live with that?"

I told him I could.

"Go talk to Coach Belichick and convey your heart to him."

That spring of 2015, Magleby brokered a meeting for me with Mike Friday, the national Men's Sevens head coach who'd be coaching the Olympic side. Friday started coaching the US Sevens team in 2014. He'd been a national head coach previously, for England and Kenya. Friday had seen highlights of me in the College Rugby Championships in 2010 and 2011. But Friday grew up in England, was not an NFL fan, and knew nothing of the Patriots' success. You could forgive him for wondering about the motivations of someone who'd left rugby years before and now, a year before the Olympics, wanted to return.

Friday was skeptical. He'd been told to "take a look at" lots of athletes over the years. Most didn't amount to much. I'd have been skeptical, too. Nor did I want or expect any favors. I really didn't want special treatment as "the NFL guy."

"You can train with us. I saw you in college, you looked pretty good," Friday said to me. It was a courtesy meeting for him. That was fine with me. If he's immediately high on me, he's disrespecting the players already on the national Sevens team. I didn't need praise or encouragement. Just a slightly opened door.

Friday said he'd let me train with the national Sevens once the Patriots season ended. On January 23, 2016, what would have been my dad's sixty-first birthday, we lost in the AFC title game to the Denver Broncos. In early March, I talked on the phone with Bill Belichick about a new contract. "There's one more thing," I said.

I explained it all to him: my dream, my dad, my determination to give the Olympics a shot. "I understand if you don't want to give me a new contract. But this is something I have to do." I loved the Patriots organization. I respected Bill. The Pats ethos mirrored my own, and they'd valued my intangibles from the day they drafted me. I was in as good a spot in my football career as I could be. But I was not going to let the love of my life get away.

Belichick was all for it. "Hell, yes," he said. "I know how much this means to you." He knew about my relationship with my dad, and what it would have meant to him. Bill is also a very patriotic guy. He has been known to quiz rookies on the meaning of June 6, 1944, and to rip them when they didn't know it was the date of the D-Day landings in World War II.

"Is there any significance to this day?" he'd ask rookies in minicamp on Memorial Day. Bill's dad, Steve, was a legendary scout while coaching football at the Naval Academy. Bill grew up around the flag.

"You have a chance to represent your country. Make us proud," he said. I had to agree to one stipulation: If I got hurt playing rugby, the contract would be voided. As Bill put it, "It's not like you're going sailing." I avoided free agency and signed a two-year extension with the Patriots. I could make a run at the Games with a clear head.

I don't know if Bill would have been so agreeable had one of our "stars" made such a request. Rob Gronkowski might not have been green-lighted so quickly. It didn't matter. It wouldn't have mattered if Bill had said no. I was going to make a run at the Olympics. By the winter of 2015–16, I could see absolutely no reason not to.

Rugby had me. It always had. Rugby was my father, and my father's spirit floated over everything I did. So much of who I am is wrapped up in this simple, beautiful game, played by men to whom honor and humility were more than concepts.

That I'd be competing to be an Olympian made the quest downright surreal. How many people can say they've played two sports at the highest level? It was like chasing rainbows when I already had a pot of gold. Consider the circumstances. Rugby hadn't been an Olympic sport since 1924. It returned when I was in my athletic prime. The US wasn't even supposed to qualify for the Olympics. We did. The stars seemed aligned.

I love football. It has given me a purpose, it has offered the biggest stage for the ultimate expression of who I am. Football has honored my hard work and validated my striving in a way no other career could.

I don't love it like I love rugby.

Football is a dear friend. We've been through a lot together. I appreciate what it has done for me. But football nags at the edges of my heart. It will never own it.

It was rugby that built the relationship with my dad, rep by rep. Rugby that my dad used as a podium for his life lectures. *Finish strong, Eb.* . . . Rugby that defined him and gave him purpose and joy. *The only game where you can beat the shit out of someone and not get arrested.* . . .

When I was dying daily in the weight room at six a.m., trying to make the football team at Ohio State, Jeff Ebner had already made his premature exit. When I struggled with the Patriots to keep the promise alive, he was watching from some distant seat I could only wonder about.

When I was ten, I was lugging the dirty water jug to his rugby practice. At thirteen, I was playing alongside him. It was real, not some hope or wish that never went anywhere. Football was a means to an end. Rugby was a calling.

It kept me up at night. I didn't *want* to play rugby in the Olympics. I absolutely needed it. Rugby was an Ebner heirloom, handed down from father to son. What a tribute to that love the Olympics would be.

Even if I didn't make the team, the attempt would suffice to ease my mind. Love isn't practical. We do best what we feel down deep. The heart wants what the heart wants.

To the vast majority of Americans who don't know much about rugby or that the US even had a team in the 2016 Games, all this might have seemed over the top, even a little reckless. To those who knew me longest and best, it was preordained.

I like playing rugby more than football. The camaraderie is special. I could go to a rugby bar in New Zealand and feel as welcome as I would in Ohio. My Olympic teammate Danny Barrett called rugby "the biggest small community in the world."

In the cutthroat NFL, we're all independent contractors and we know why NFL means Not For Long. The time to nurture close bonds isn't there.

In the NFL, we take two-hour plane trips ten times a year. In the rugby World Series, we spend a month on the road together, all over the world. New Zealand-to-Sydney-to-Los Angeles-to-Vancouver-to-Hong Kong-to-Singapore. And so on. Rugby owns my best memories, from traveling the world and around the country, to just being in Ohio with my dad.

I like the rugby culture. It has a blue-collar appeal and I like to think I have blue-collar sensibilities. Jeff Ebner wore a blue collar to work every day. Most rugby players in this country are workaday people like the guys at Scioto Valley Rugby Club. They pay to play. Their payoff is in their experiences.

Rugby owns a genuineness I like. Guys without bullshit working hard and playing hard, living for their families and loyal to their friends. They're not frat boys in the financial industry with their boat shoes on.

No one is better than the next guy. No pretense, no frauds, no entitlement. I don't understand entitlement. At the Olympics, we had a No Dickhead rule. If you thought you were bigger than the team, we didn't need you. Everybody sweats the same in rugby. Everybody dies a little from exhaustion and hurts a little from the collisions. It doesn't matter who you think you are.

Wins and losses stay on the pitch. You get knocked down, you get helped up. Referees are addressed as sir or ma'am. If you curse a ref, you're out of the match. Mike Friday can't recall anyone ever doing it. In this way, you could almost compare rugby to golf. It's civil, it's collegial, the humility it fosters has been passed down through the ages. You can be a brute when it's called for. You don't have to be a jerk in the process.

There are frauds in football. You see one every time a defensive player lays out a defenseless receiver, then stands over him like he's done something special. The next play, that same tough guy will shy from a big running back barreling through the hole right at him.

In rugby, everyone can tackle. Everyone has to tackle. Everyone has to do everything: run, pass, catch, kick, tackle. In football, the best offensive lineman in the world would be the worst quarterback in the league.

I laugh when I hear NFL players talk about playing seventy

or seventy-five downs in a game. The fact is, if you're, say, a defensive back, you might be directly involved in a handful of those plays. In rugby, you're involved all the time, because the game constantly moves.

Rugby shape is different than football shape. That's something I had to relearn when I jumped back into the sport. Football is a game of starts and stops. Rugby—especially Sevens rugby—is balls-out for two seven-minute halves. Or, in Fifteens, a constant pace for eighty minutes.

Alex Magleby said, "Sevens is a fourteen-minute fury, no rest. It's like running four hundred meters, doing ten squat jumps, then wrestling a bear. Rest three hours, repeat. Five [matches] in a day."

Fifteens is the movie. Sevens is the trailer. Put in basketball terms, Fifteens is like half-court five-on-five. Sevens is full court three-on-three. If you're talking about the structure and flow of Sevens, basketball is the best comparison. Speed and space are your biggest concerns.

Think about running down on kickoffs continuously for seven minutes. You have to be in the best shape of your life to play rugby, especially Sevens. Run, tackle, get up, run, tackle again. Make split-second decisions when you're exhausted. You don't have enough energy to speak. Where do I enter the ruck? Where do I pass? Run with the ball, or kick it? If I run, do I go left or right, or straight through?

In Sevens, you can be spent and the game isn't over. You go to some dark places in Sevens matches.

I like rugby's flow. Football can be robotic and overcoached.

We watch more film in football than your average movie critic. I watch it because it makes me better prepared and, by extension, more valuable on the field. But I can't say I love the overanalysis of the game.

Rugby is a player's game. There is no time to analyze, and the game moves too quickly to call plays. The biggest in-game decision a Sevens coach will make is when to sub out an exhausted player. Again, rugby is like basketball that way. You can't sit there and analyze every dribble Steph Curry takes. Football coaches analyze every step you take. Literally. Footwork, footwork, footwork.

With rugby, there is never a moment that happens exactly how you were taught. Improvisation is allowed to thrive, within the flow.

Rugby is not as hard on my body as football, even with the constant confrontations. They're both collision sports. Football more so, if only because the tackles tend to be more direct and head on. Rugby doesn't allow you simply to zero in on a ballcarrier. You have to defend players who don't have the ball. Rugby emphasizes efficient tackling.

Football stops and starts. You're asked to change direction abruptly, and to backpedal. Every move is as explosive as you can make it. That's hard on your joints.

I have to maintain a constant energy in rugby, but at the end of a game or practice, my joints aren't sore. The morning after, I don't have that hit-by-a-truck experience. I haven't taken a face mask to the forearm or had my toes stepped on by a 350-pound lineman. My head didn't get smashed, my shoulders weren't strained. I ran a lot, so my hamstrings are sore. I didn't take a helmet to the thigh.

As one writer suggested, "Football is rugby's sociopathic younger brother, hell-bent on destruction and colossal collisions."

I didn't get concussed playing rugby, even though I wasn't wearing a helmet. Rugby doesn't permit tackling above the shoulders. You can't have multiple players running full blast at the guy with the ball. If you do, your defense is going to have huge holes. You have to work together. That can't involve gang tackling.

Your body doesn't suffer one big wreck in rugby. It wears out, like a pickup truck at two hundred thousand miles. It's the nature of the contact. Worn-out knees, hairline rib fractures, cauliflower ears, what the NFL lists on its injury reports as "general soreness." Rugby is harder in the moment. I can't catch my breath, I have to think on my feet, I can't stop.

The Olympics were made for me. Long odds and a short time to prepare. Unlikely, but not impossible. I was familiar with that turf. At Ohio State, I competed against the best amateur football players in the country. In the Olympics, I would compete against the best Sevens players in the world. If I made the team. Rugby had given me a lot. Now I could return the favor.

Six weeks after the Patriots lost to the Denver Broncos, I was in a dorm room at the Olympic Training Center in Chula Vista, California, just outside San Diego. Preparing for a World Cup event in Hong Kong. And so began the time of my life.

I left rugby for practicality. Six years later, I returned for love.

NINETEEN

Yaka Yards

Trying out for the Olympics came straight from my heart and was not negotiable. Love is commitment and commitment is the willingness to sacrifice everything for something you want. I believed that. I lived it. It was a big, defining personal experiment that had never failed. But it had never tested me the way I would be tested between March and July 2016.

It was as if I were a Patriots rookie listening to Scotty O'Brien all over again. *Ebner, you don't know what you don't know.* I knew returning to elite-level rugby wouldn't be easy. I didn't want it to be. What I didn't know was it would put me through everything I could handle, then ask me for a little more.

You could call it overcoming long odds. Practically speaking, you'd be right. I wanted to be one of fourteen Olympic rugby team members, including two alternates. I was competing against people who played rugby full-time, with the national team or professionally overseas. A few had been around close to a decade. They trained every day. I trained every day, too, but not for rugby.

Their skills were sharp. They were in good rugby shape. I was conditioned for football. Eight years earlier, I was "that rugby guy" trying to play college football. Now, I was "that football guy" trying to play rugby.

I'd been away from football for five years when I walked on at Ohio State. I'd been gone from rugby for six. Time away wasn't the issue, though. My formative rugby years were in high school and college. I wouldn't have to relearn rugby, just rediscover it. The on-the-job training as a walk-on football player was far more intense.

But long odds? Long odds are winning the Powerball or beating Stage 4 cancer. People can't control how their immune systems respond. I've had a say in everything I've done. The decisions have been mine. I've controlled most of the outcomes. I haven't bemoaned my luck or waited for it to change. If I've had good luck, it has been with the mostly good health I've enjoyed.

Some people are blessed with physical gifts. They're "born" to succeed. Others are born without sight or the ability to walk. Between those extremes is the huge middle ground, where we have a say in our lives based on the effort we invest.

I know how much I'm willing to sacrifice compared with other people. I know it's always possible for me to get what I want. Long odds and genetic blessings have nothing to do with it.

Two weeks after the Patriots lost the AFC title game, Mike

Friday sent me the national rugby team's training regimen. I read it with some astonishment. "No way. Nobody's doing these numbers. That pace, with that little rest," I said. I did not know.

I could not have imagined practicing three times a day. Football practice is two or three hours a day, one time. Mike Friday had us running 5,000 meters each practice, three practices a day. That's almost 5,500 yards per workout, more than 16,000 yards total. Football players never do more than about 4,000 yards in a practice.

Workouts on the rowing machines were equally draining: Meeting the rugby demand—45-second splits at a 1:35 or 1:40 pace, with 15 seconds rest in between, for 10 sets—was daunting. When we weren't sprinting, we'd do 10,000-meter races between two teams, rotating guys as we got tired. The losers had to do more conditioning.

And that's not counting the Yaka Yards.

Friday also made it plain he wasn't impressed with my Patriots pedigree. "You're not getting any favors because you're an NFL boy," he said. Fine. I didn't want any.

The Olympic Training Center in Chula Vista, California—now known as the Chula Vista Elite Athlete Training Center—is 155 acres devoted to building better Olympians. Track-and-field athletes train there. So do archers, cyclists, Paralympians, and Sevens rugby players, among others.

When the rugby team wasn't touring the globe as a member of the Rugby Sevens Series, it trained in Chula Vista. I moved into a dorm-style apartment at the center in mid-March.

The training center sits on an idyllic piece of property seven miles south of San Diego. Rolling hills, lakes, well-manicured practice fields, perfect weather. Quiet and peaceful and distraction-free. Its great looks are cosmetic. They don't reveal what's actually happening on the grounds. Specifically, significant pain on the rugby pitch.

My first week at the center, I trained with young, developmental guys. These were players ages seventeen through twenty-two who needed more exposure to high-level rugby. They were rugby's version of the NFL's practice squad.

My legs were so heavy, I felt like I was running in glue. A coach told me to pick it up. "You're creating a gap" in the line, he said. Gaps in the line are a mortal rugby sin. That was my first indication I wasn't at football practice anymore. Rugby is an on-going aerobic torture, mixed with hard physical contact. I wasn't ready for that.

Sevens rugby is a whole different animal. It's fourteen minutes of relentless fury. You have to psych yourself up to perform at the highest possible level for fourteen minutes, then calm that emotion, rehydrate, and let the brain regenerate before playing the next match two hours later. In a Series event, you're doing that six times in two days.

The conditioning mimics the matches. Ideally, you get to where you're thinking only about playing rugby, not about how much your heart and lungs hate you. Friday had any number of ways to get us to that point.

There were the five-meter up downs. Two cones, five meters

apart. Thirty seconds. A whistle blows, you run five meters, do an up down, run back five meters do an up down. That's one rep. You try to get six reps in thirty seconds, with thirty seconds rest between sets. The first time we did this, I didn't even finish a complete set of six. By the end of the Olympic camp, I was one of just a few who hit all six for all six sets. That didn't help me in March. I was running drills and thinking, *I can't even pick my legs up.*

My body was nowhere near the point where I could push it the way I would need to. I was behind on everything. Catching up would take time. I wondered if I had enough.

My first competition in six years would come in Hong Kong. We played the Series events in pairs. Hong Kong and Singapore were first, then Paris and London. We'd train a week in between each event. When we finished in London, we flew back to Chula Vista for three or four weeks of training.

Hong Kong and Singapore let me know my status quickly. I was as close to making the Olympic Sevens team as I was to replacing Tom Brady as the Patriots' quarterback. Two issues arose:

I was playing rugby with a football sensibility, and I didn't understand how Mike Friday wanted our team to play. He wanted us to wear teams down by stretching them back and forth across the pitch. They get tired, they drift out of position. Their lines are easier to attack.

Attacking the correct space and running the correct lines go hand in hand. You can't do one without the other. Everything on offense is about attacking space.

Also, not being in rugby shape complicated things. Part of the battle is playing at a high level when you're exhausted. I needed to be in good enough shape that I wasn't worried about blowing myself out in the first couple minutes of the second half. These weren't trivial matters. I battled them for months, right up to the beginning of the Olympic tryout camp in June.

As I've said, when it comes to constant motion and flow, and using movement to find a gap in the defense, Sevens has more in common with basketball than with football. I played a little hoops in high school, junior varsity mostly, enough to see the similarities.

In my years away from rugby, I worked in the regimented football worlds of Ohio State University and the New England Patriots. I lived in a Bill Belichick state of mind: Don't screw up. That had to change.

Sevens rugby is free-flowing and instinctual. Football is marching music. Rugby is jazz. In rugby, there's no time to ponder, only to anticipate, react, and trust your skills. Thinking costs you speed. Imagine if LeBron James actually thought about every dribble and step he took. Like basketball, good rugby has to be played freely. It didn't help that I was playing in a system foreign to me, with new teammates, and I was trying to do it at the highest level. The learning curve was dramatic.

I underestimated the conditioning required. I expected to be one of the best-conditioned players on the team, even if that meant dying a little in the weight room and on the pitch. I was familiar with that sort of pain. It was temporary. This was harder than that. The pain was mandatory. And by itself, not enough.

In international Sevens, the fitness level is through the roof. You need a different mindset to endure it. We called the most extreme workouts Yaka Yards. Training makes you yak. Throw up. A forty-five-minute cardio session without a break produces a line of players zombie-crawling off the pitch while relieving their stomachs of their contents.

No one knows for sure where the term comes from. Some say Fiji. Others say Mike Friday and assistant coach Chris Brown brought it from Kenya, where they'd previously coached the Kenyan national team. That would be appropriate, given the number of yaks their training sessions induced. Personally, I gave credit to Folau Niua, our longest-tenured Sevens team member. He's Polynesian. It sounds like something he'd say.

Yaka Yards workouts served two masters. One was the obvious purpose of getting in rugby shape. The other was more subtle and equally important: thickening the mental calluses required to finish the training session. Yaka Yards workouts can break you physically, at least for a short time. The mental impact can be longer lasting. Dreading Yaka Yards can be worse than experiencing them.

Rugby people have another saying to describe the mental fist-fight between what Anthony Schlegel labeled the selfish and inner beasts: the Dark Place. That's the little acreage of hell every Sevens player visits at times. It's where your heart and lungs have exceeded their limitations and can help you no more. It's what drowning must feel like.

The Dark Place descends most often late in a match, when

you're in your twelfth or thirteenth minute of running and tack-ling. It's not physically possible to take another step, yet the clock says two minutes still remain. The lactic acid spews fire, the brain fogs. I loved Jeff Ebner's exhortations, but in the midst of all this drowning and burning up, I couldn't remember what they were.

The little voice that lives in the Dark Place is real. He's telling me I'm physically gone. The longer you're in the Dark Place, the louder the voice gets.

Mike Friday's theory was simple: When you've been to the Dark Place in training, it's less of a shock when you experience it in a game. You can concentrate on thinking, not stomach erup-tions. You need to get comfortable with being uncomfortable.

During a Sevens match, you catch your breath in the middle of a dead sprint. Make a tackle, get back in the game, and "re-cover" until the next contact. That's why the drills were perpet-ual. Full exhaustion for forty-five minutes, minus six to eight minutes of rest.

Yaka Yards and Dark Place trips were frequent during high-performance training sessions. *High performance* was a term for any top-level training involving the "A-side" of US Sevens. Olym-pic camp was a high-performance camp. So was every training camp before a Series event. There is simply no way to detail the intensity of these workouts, unless you've experienced them. I can only try to paint an adequate picture.

We did "reloads." They were down/ups, with contact. Run, hit the ground, get up, hit a tackle bag or a pad with another player pushing you back.

We did RSDs, repeated sprints for distance. They were similar to shuttle runs. Cones at five-meter intervals up to thirty meters. Up to the cone and back, up to the next cone and back. Thirty seconds to finish the set. Repeat. We did bear crawls, a minute at a time, with a partner hanging beneath us, by our necks. And so on.

Visiting the Dark Place never gets easier. During the Olympic camp, we were there almost every day. You knew it was coming, it was inevitable, so ideally you were able to deal with it mentally. I went to the Dark Place so often, I almost got used to it. I became better at fighting the pain. The more I visited, the longer it would take the voice to come calling. Regardless, if you're not experiencing Darkness in practice, you're probably not going to be effective in the game.

As Anthony Schlegel would explain it, "You're going to find out a lot about yourself in blood, sweat, and pain. The selfish beast says, 'I'm already faster than these guys. I'm already in better shape. I can slow down.' Either you handle it, ignore the voice, and tap into your inner beast, or you don't."

The mind wants you to give up before the body does. Get back in the game.

For my first rugby tournament in six years I was chosen to play for a select team called Samurai, in the Hong Kong Tens. The Tens is a ten-a-side tournament begun in 1986, to honor the one hundredth season of the Hong Kong Football Club. The Tens tournament was on Wednesday and Thursday of the week, with the Sevens Series on Friday, Saturday, and Sunday.

It was a baptism by fire. We played six games in two days in an impossible, steamy heat. I didn't need a reminder of how rugby tests your physical limits and makes you feel like quitting every time you play. I got one, anyway.

Samurai made it to the championship game. Day 2, Game 6. It was 0–0 after regulation time. I lost a contact lens during the game. I played with a bruised hand I'd had surgery on two months earlier. The match went to double overtime. I'd never tackled so much in my life. We lost 5–0 on a bad lineout the other team converted into a try.

I dressed for the Sevens event over the weekend, but I was too beat up to play. I did make some points with Mike Friday, though. He said he admired my resilience, and that I'd given him a glimpse of my potential, if I could play myself into shape and stop thinking like a football player.

I played prop in Singapore the next week. That's a position in the front row of the scrum, usually played by someone bigger than I am. Because Sevens (unlike Fifteens) is a game of speed and agility over size and strength, props are not the force they are in Fifteens. They ruck, hit, and pass the ball to the backs, mostly. Friday played me at prop because it's a little easier defensively than center, my normal spot, and I was big enough to handle the position.

In Sevens, though, you play your best players, with only a little regard to the positions they play. Props do score, but the speed of the game means the outside guys get most of the tries.

I weighed about 210; the props I was playing against were 230.

Once they started leaning on me, I got tired in a hurry. My skills were rusty even when I was fresh. In fact, I thought the way I played in Singapore was disgusting. I had a long way to go.

Meantime, I was dealing with uncomfortable publicity. Hotshot football player, trying to be an Olympian. An ESPN reporter was a regular in Chula Vista. It was embarrassing for me. I hadn't done a thing to earn the attention. I did all the media and absorbed the good-natured crap I took from my teammates. I was grateful it was good-natured. In a way, the undeserved hype made me work harder. I didn't want my teammates saying, "Who does this guy think he is?"

They weren't used to being noticed, even as they traveled the world. The team would run into fellow Americans occasionally, somewhere along the Capetown/Dubai/Vancouver circuit. When the players explained who they were and what they did, the reaction was typically, "The US has a rugby team?"

I thought if I could bring some attention to the sport I loved, we'd all benefit. I didn't want to take anyone's shine, but the truth was, USA Rugby needed the notebooks and cameras. I clipped any potential resentment by exhausting myself every day. I was serious about making the team, not about making myself famous.

Paris was our next stop. I played ten minutes total in five games. I knew the problems. I still believed I could overcome them. But it was early May. Olympic camp was barely a month away. I had to start turning Mike Friday's head.

I wasn't in shape yet. I wasn't aware of my positioning on the field. That awareness should have come naturally for me, but I was tired. When you're tired, you don't think clearly. In Sevens, you can't be out of position. Games usually are close enough that one breakdown, one bad moment, can cost you a win. Friday explained it best: "You can't make mistakes in Sevens. The game is too fast. Nate made mistakes. He wouldn't make a pass when he needed to, he wouldn't find the right space to attack. He was too conservative. That's an error in our game."

Our captain, Madison Hughes, said, "It took a while for the game to slow down for him. The game has its own rhythm and flow. In football, you execute a plan. In rugby, you react to a flow."

Every time I caught the ball I was thinking, *Don't make a mistake*. You can't play rugby like that. As a ballcarrier, I'd think twice about skinning a guy (beating him around the edge) because I wasn't sure I could make it. If I didn't get around the corner, I wouldn't score and get the brief rest that happens after scoring a try. You second-guess how to go at people when you're not fit enough to do what you want.

The frustrating part was, I knew I could play. The right stuff was in there. Here was Alex Magleby's evaluation of me at the time:

Nate is fast, he moves well laterally, he understands the concept of space, how to create it and use it. He's superb technically with his passes. He can ruck well, he can tackle, he's a good decision maker, a coach on the field. He's an old head and an old soul, who could positively impact the younger guys. If he wasn't playing in the NFL, he'd be the national team's starting center.

After the Paris tournament, Mike Friday gave me a choice.

I could go on to London with the Eagles (our A-side) and not play much, or I could accept a demotion of sorts and play with our B-side, the Falcons, in Tours, France, where I would play every minute and have more chances to rediscover my rugby self.

Friday evaluated me at that point. "Nate's chances hadn't improved much. He was still struggling with the transition from the collisions of the NFL to managing the contact in rugby. He was relearning how to manage and manipulate space. He needed more time on the pitch, to resurrect those memories so they'd be second nature. Essentially, we needed to start seeing Rugby Nate."

There was something else. I needed to find my Fuck It and get it back on. The Jeff Ebner approach. Just let it go. I did it eventually in my rookie year with the Patriots. Two weeks in Tours with the B team would give me time to relax and just play rugby. I felt like I was on the outside looking in. I also knew who I was, and what I was capable of. It was all up to me. That was all I could ask for.

"Does Tours give me the best chance to make the Olympics?" I asked Friday.

"Yes, it does."

I went with the Falcons to Tours.

Before sending me off, Friday encouraged me to "stop worrying about making mistakes. You're playing too hesitant. Go to Tours. More playing time, less pressure. Just play."

He praised my humility for accepting the demotion. After all, the players called Tours "fake Paris." But it wasn't humility. It was a practical decision. I wasn't getting better because I wasn't playing enough. I couldn't find Rugby Nate on the sideline. At that juncture, I'd have played for the Falcons, the Eagles, or a bunch of parakeets if it meant I'd be on the field.

I would go to this random tournament in the middle of French nowhere and play my ass off, unchained, and, in so doing, get my mind right. "We had to let him make mistakes," said Friday. "You have to get it wrong to get it right."

I was on a mission at Tours. I said to myself, *It's not working the way you're doing it. Just say fuck it and try to crush everyone across from you. Stop giving the other guys so much respect. Have a go every time you touch the ball.*

I can't say exactly what happened after that. I was working myself into rugby shape. The more fit I became, the clearer my thinking was on the field. The mental game improved. I started to let the game happen, feel the flow, remember the beauty and why I loved playing rugby. Mike Friday explained it better: "His body was rounding into form, so we could start focusing on his mind."

As I said, I was not relearning rugby. That knowledge was always there. I was rediscovering it. The timing that drives the choreography involved in attacking a line. Knowing which lines to attack, seeing where the space is. Running without the ball to manipulate a defender, similar to a three-on-two fast break in basketball. Catching the ball at full speed. Learning my teammates' tendencies and syncing with them.

I needed Tours to ditch all the junk in my head that was holding me back. It felt like my old Ohio State rugby days. I just had a go every time I had the ball. I don't want to cliché-it by saying "the lightbulb went on." I might have underestimated the challenges of returning to elite rugby after a six-year hiatus. That's what happened when I walked on at OSU. I'd never underestimated my ability to get anything I wanted, if I worked for it. And I wasn't so prideful I wouldn't question what I was doing.

Beyond that? Desperation was a great motivator.

"Nate knew the game," Friday explained years later. "After (six) years, it was in the back of his mind. We had to get it to the front of his mind."

Friday also said, privately, to others at the time: "I don't think Nate's gonna make it."

BETWEEN TWENTY-FIVE AND THIRTY of us received an invite to Olympic camp, which started in early June. This was the situation the day we started camp:

Several players were all but assured of spots, guys who'd played on the national team for several years: Danny Barrett; Folau Niua; Martin Iosefo; the captain, Madison Hughes; Carlin Isles, the fastest man in rugby; and Perry Baker, who would be named Sevens Player of the Year in the two seasons after the Olympics. Zack Test had played more matches internationally (been "capped," in rugby lingo) than any US Sevens player ever. At that point, he'd also scored more trys than any American. Garrett Bender and Maka Unufe were veterans. A few youngsters would get serious consideration: Ben Pinkelman and Steve Tomasin. And me.

Nearly all of us would walk into Maracanã Stadium in Rio, two months later. In between was a test for which I'd been preparing my whole life. Officially, the fight to make the Olympic team commenced the first week of June 2016 in Chula Vista. Unofficially, it originated in the weight room behind the garage in Springfield, Ohio, two decades before. Everything I'd ever done was a prelude to what I was about to do.

The Tours gamble paid off. In fact, it was one of the best career decisions I've ever made. Everything before Olympic tryout camp was about keeping up, keeping it together, getting my conditioning right so my brain could direct my body even when I was exhausted.

I came to camp in good rugby shape. My body was rounding into form. So was my mind. The confidence I'd regained in Tours restored my Fuck It. My game was falling in line. Rugby Nate was back.

If I didn't make the Olympic team, it wouldn't be because I didn't give myself the chance.

Olympic camp was strictly high performance. Six days a week, three sessions a day. Weight lifting, cardio conditioning, tactical and technical drills, scrimmaging. Pain. All under the judgmental eyes of Mike Friday. Steve Tomasin put it like this:

"Every time we'd walk to practice I'd say, 'Let the physical beating go. Shut your brain off and let your legs and lungs work. If you don't accept pain, someone else will. Put your head down. Grind.'"

I'd use that ten-minute walk to get my mind right. We all

would. Down a path of smooth, cobbled stones surrounded by freshly planted trees, in the eight a.m. chill before the sun took over. That was the time to get it together. The pain was coming. No use fighting it. Remember what you're fighting for.

Unless you were one of the team's established veterans—Hughes, Barrett, Isles, Baker, Test, Niua, a few others—each session could make or break your chances of earning a spot. Eighteen to twenty guys were good enough to make the team.

Every day had three sessions; each lasted between sixty and ninety minutes. One always involved the weight room, the others were on the field.

One type of scrimmaging, called Chaos, was full-speed, non-contact touch rugby. It was continuous. If the ball went out of touch (out of bounds), a coach would just toss in a new one. It was chaos, literally.

I needed everything I'd ever learned about conditioning to survive Olympic camp. That little voice in your head is real. You have to be prepared to shout it down. I needed Jeff Ebner's angel on my shoulder, urging me to finish strong while repeating his promise to me that if I could conquer my pain, my glory would last forever. I needed Schlegel's intensity to slay my selfish beast and feed him to my inner beast. I needed Belichick's obsession riding shotgun next to my own. Even with all that positive expertise, I had my down moments. Three weeks into camp, on my second day of three-a-days, I was toasted. I called my mom.

"Remind me of this conversation if I ever say I want to do this again," I said. "I'm not going to quit. I've come too far. But this is insane." I'm not a whiner. I whined. I knew about crazy workouts. I'd survived the Ohio State walk-on tryout, whose only purpose was to scare us off. I made it through the endless slog of my first and second years in the NFL.

This was a new level of anguish. You put me in a mental toughness challenge with anyone, I'll bet on myself. But at the Olympic camp, I've got people like that all around me.

In the years after the '16 Games, everyone would agree the training was overdone. Some guys would suggest we had peaked too soon, before the Olympics started. By the time we played Argentina in our first match in Rio, we were already overcooked. Mike Friday believed we needed a tough camp, but he would say afterward that training for the 2020 Games would involve less conditioning.

I persevered. We all did. This was for the Olympics. Friday said he saw an uptick in my confidence. I was attacking lines and making good decisions, with and without the ball. He also told Nigel Melville three weeks into camp, "I'm not taking this guy just because he's a Patriot."

On July 23, the team went to a San Diego Padres baseball game. The Olympic roster would be announced via email, at nine that night. We stayed for part of the game. Some of the guys left to celebrate the end of camp. I went back to my room and refreshed my in-box and saw my name.

I had made the Olympic team.

I allowed myself a moment. It was a familiar, brief elation before my mind shifted to balling out in Rio. I'd done what I'd said I was going to do. When I first got to Chula Vista five months earlier, I could barely keep up with practice. By July 23, I was one of the fittest players on the team.

I didn't know it, but Friday had decided two days earlier that I would make the team. "I couldn't keep him off it," he said years later. He added that by the end of camp I was one of the best players on the side. Friday also recounted that I needed to be that good, because he was sensitive to any charge that my appearance on the roster was for publicity as much as performance. I figured it was a last-minute call, even as I'd always thought I'd make it. I would make it as one of two centers. My main job was to get the ball and pass it to Perry on the outside.

Mike Friday said of my odyssey, "I look back and wonder how he did it. He didn't complain. He was winded and tired. By the end of a Sevens match, you're exhausted, desperate for air, and trying to think and communicate. Mix in the collisions. Getting off the floor and back in the game gets harder and harder. And that's for the guys who are in shape. Nate wasn't in shape."

I needed everything I'd ever learned to make that team. I won't say that my life to that point had been one long run-up to that email in my in-box. I'll just say that I was going to Rio de Janeiro to represent the United States in the 2016 Olympic Summer Games.

Fucking right.

TWENTY

All in the Family

Folau Niua was a streetwise, drug-dealing teenager from East Palo Alto, California, which is nothing like its wealthy brother Palo Alto, home to Stanford University and million-dollar fixer-uppers. In 1992, the FBI named East Palo Alto the murder capital of America. A few days into his first season with a newly formed rugby club in his neighborhood, Folau got arrested for fighting and missed the whole year.

Carlin Isles and his twin sister saw their mother taken away in a police vehicle in Akron, Ohio, when they were six. They spent the next few years in foster homes. Carlin ran his way out of potential trouble, literally. He was a sprinter in high school and college who dreamed of challenging Usain Bolt in the 2012 Games. He ran 40 yards in 4.22 seconds. He would come to be known as "the fastest man in rugby."

Perry Baker aspired to be a homicide detective, a dream hatched after the murder of one of his young friends went unsolved.

Danny Barrett's nickname is Beast. Find some video online, you'll see the nickname fits. But Madison Hughes, all 175 pounds of him, could bring the Beast to the ground.

Zack Test played on the wing. We were teammates on the U-19 team in Ireland and then on the U-20 team that played in Wales. No one could have predicted we'd be back on the same side nearly a decade later. Zack held the team record for tries in the Sevens Series until 2018, when Perry Baker overtook him. Like Carlin and Perry, Zack started college as a football player. He was a preferred walk-on as a freshman at Oregon, but didn't get any playing time. The next year, he transferred to Loughborough University, Salty Thompson's alma mater, to concentrate on rugby. Zack retired in 2018.

These were my teammates in Rio de Janeiro.

I had to get used to them, they had to get used to me. We had to hit a stride together. It wasn't easy. In retrospect, we didn't quite get there. Strong and different personalities don't come together instantly. Since 2016 Mike Friday has devoted a lot of time to relationship building. Trust can be as important as talent in our sport. Trust takes time.

Some sides are together for years, especially in places such as New Zealand, where players make a decent living playing rugby. Other places, such as Fiji, the money isn't great, but rugby is the national sport. The status conferred keeps players and teams together. The US is a team of talented individuals in comparison.

America lacks the built-in advantages of good pay and prestige, and so, in a sport so dependent on selflessness and teamwork, the team is made up of people who don't get to spend a tremendous amount of time together.

And whose backgrounds couldn't be any more different: A Polynesian (Folau) passes to a former football player (Perry) who passes to a would-be track star (Carlin) who hands off to a current NFL player (me). All follow the lead of their 175-pound captain (Madison), who at the time was the leading tackler in the history of the Sevens World Series.

Nobody had the same story, but a couple themes dominated. Desperation was one. Folau was a high school dropout when a former rugby player named Rob Holder decided to form the East Palo Alto club for at-risk kids. For Holder, it was social work with some coaching thrown in.

Folau had rugby experience. The kid Rob Holder saw had great hands, was athletic, could kick, and was competitive. Holder learned more when Folau came out again, in his second season, only to injure his right knee. He turned that newest disappointment into an opportunity. Naturally a left-footed kicker, Folau used his right foot as his plant foot. While getting his knee healthy, he also learned to kick with his right foot while planting with his left. When Folau returned to full health, he could kick with both feet. That's a huge advantage in Sevens.

He committed to staying out of trouble the night before games. As Holder bluntly explained, "Folau dealt drugs." In that neighborhood, he wasn't alone. Holder installed Folau at fly half, a position that requires clear thinking, good decision making, and good passing and kicking skills. Think of a point guard in basketball.

The more success Folau had, the less trouble he found. By 2011, he'd made the US national Sevens team. He's still there almost a decade later, "the glue of the team" in Barrett's words, who has played in more Sevens matches than any American. Folau also kicks off for us. The kickoff is the most important play in Sevens, because it determines possession. Folau is great at it. The ball has to go at least ten meters and it should be high enough to give the kicking team a chance to run under it.

Think of it like an onside kick in football. In Sevens, all kickoffs are onside kicks.

Meanwhile, Carlin Isles had run out of athletic options when he happened upon some rugby video online. He had played football and run track in high school and at Ashland University in Ohio. He'd had a good college career in both, but not good enough to make a living at either.

He was online looking for a track club that might need a sprinter when he saw the rugby video. "That might be something I could do," he said.

Carlin had a rough early childhood, but he wasn't a rough kid. When he was seven, Charles and Starlett Isles legally adopted him and his sister. Carlin cut out stories of athletes who'd gotten in trouble and pasted the stories on his bedroom wall as warnings.

In high school, he ran 40 yards in 4.28 seconds. At Ashland, he held school records in the 100 and 200 meters and had a 100-yard kickoff return. Before he found rugby in 2012, Carlin ran a personal-best time of 10.24 seconds in the 100 meters, the thirty-sixth-fastest 100 time in the US that year.

Carlin emailed Nigel Melville, then president of USA Rugby. Melville set him up with a club team in Aspen, Colorado. Carlin packed everything he owned into his used Hyundai Sonata and drove to Colorado. He had $500 to his name and he needed $250 of that for gas. He was twenty-two years old.

It didn't take long for his speed to turn heads. *Rugby Magazine* called him "the fastest man in American rugby." He debuted for the national Sevens team in October 2012 and scored a try in his first minute on the pitch. Carlin also looked at trying to qualify for the '12 Olympics, but the Trials coincided with rugby training camp. A chance to challenge the great Bolt was less important to him than developing a career he believed was his future.

Carlin couldn't make it on speed alone. With his speed and acceleration, Carlin got to top speed quickly. But at the elite level, almost everyone can run. You have to learn to use your speed. As a wing, Carlin had to learn to run with patience. Running 40 yards in 4.2 seconds didn't help his decision making.

Carlin called it "reading pictures." It's a term Mike Friday uses. The team would watch film, Friday would pause it and tell us to "look at the picture" and ask us what we saw. Teams try to take away the outside when they defend Carlin, because if he skins them, he's gone. Five points for us.

Standard Sevens defense is tight inside, with soft corners. "Soft play," we call it. Bend on defense, but defend the edge. Everyone gives ground toward the sideline, to take away the corner. The line can resemble a Slinky.

If you play the US Sevens that way, they're going to pass quickly and accurately, to skin you on the outside. In 2016, we practiced speed passing to a ridiculous extent. Carlin's job was to "read the picture," that is, see where the space was and what lines to take.

Perry Baker is Carlin without the all-world acceleration, but with a little better feel for the game. As for his overall speed, he's maybe a step slower than Carlin. Before that, he was a star wide receiver at Division II Fairmont (West Virginia) State and the nephew of four-time Pro Bowl wideout Wes Chandler. Perry signed with the Philadelphia Eagles as an undrafted free agent, but a knee injury kept him off the roster. After two years playing arena football, he started playing club rugby, then joined the Tiger Rugby Academy in Columbus, Ohio.

In Columbus, he made ends meet by working eleven-hour shifts at a pest control company and moonlighting as a security guard for a sorority at Ohio University. In 2014, he became a member of the men's Sevens team.

Isles says, "Perry's got a Kobe [Bryant] mentality. He don't fear nobody." True, but mostly, Perry knows how to play. He's fast and elusive and a good enough athlete he can play anywhere on the field. His experience as a wide receiver helps him read the pitch and set up defenders. Perry has scored more trys than any American in Sevens history. More recently, he and Carlin have become neck and neck for tries scored in each tournament.

Perry has had chances since the '16 Olympics to sign overseas for much bigger money, but he turned them down for another run at gold in Tokyo. That quest since has been delayed until the summer of 2021 by the novel coronavirus pandemic. Perry is still on board, but he will be almost thirty-five when the Games begin, so it likely will be his last shot at the medal stand.

Mike Friday has rarely paired Perry and Carlin on the pitch at the same time. It could be too much of a good thing. There's only one ball. But it would be interesting to watch defenses try to contain the fastest and the best at the same time.

Danny Barrett is nothing like Folau or Carlin. Desperation didn't drive him. He didn't face dire life circumstances, unless you count fending off his two older brothers at the dinner table. Danny was just naturally feisty.

"The smallest dog is always the last to be fed," he'd say. "You've gotta fight and scrap to get what's yours." That could explain why he and his siblings went after each other with hockey sticks growing up.

Danny and his oldest brother, Jim, were all-Americans in rugby at Cal. His other brother, Neil, was honorable mention. The three brothers all played on the same side, a first in more than 140 years of Cal rugby. Danny wears number 3, in recognition. "They have my back. They're on my back. Literally," he says.

Danny plays prop and is the biggest guy on the Sevens team. Six-three, 230 pounds. Madison Hughes calls him "the bulldozer. He'll have a clean path to the try and say, 'I think I'll trample this guy first.'" In a 2018 match against Fiji, a TV announcer described him as "a Mack truck on a skateboard."

In 2016, we had the raw talent to compete for a medal. What we didn't have—what we were trying to develop on the fly— was the sort of foxhole togetherness we needed when the competition got intense. As Mike Friday conceded a few years back, "We had a tendency to lose focus when somebody or something flew off the rails."

That can't happen in Sevens. The game is too fast, its outcomes are too close. One mistake can kill you. If you make one, get over it and get back in the game. Don't let that error lead to another. After we lost 49–0 to Argentina in Paris, we had a blowout team meeting. Lots of finger pointing. Basically, I said, "Cut the bullshit and be professionals. Take responsibility for your own performance, but remember we're a team. We win and lose together."

Mike Friday knew the importance of character development. He also knew we'd be playing in the Olympics in a few months and we weren't in shape for that. The emphasis was on the immediate need, which was the conditioning.

We arrived in Brazil in August in excellent physical condition. It was time for us to surprise the rugby world gathered in Rio de Janeiro.

TWENTY-ONE

Rio

I'm not a reflective person. Reflection requires a few things I don't do well: looking backward; pausing; feeling nostalgic. Was it better back then? I don't know. I have too much in front of me to ponder what I've left behind. Maybe when I retire.

I'd like to be able to say that on the hot and tropical night of August 5, 2016, I revisited my whole athletic life and celebrated it in my head. We certainly had time to do that. The United States team—555 Olympians in thirty-three sports—spent two hours in line, between the time we left the staging area and entered Maracanã Stadium, to join the Opening Ceremony of the XXXI Olympic Games.

Two hours shuffling in one of those zigzaggy amusement

park lines afforded me lots of time to think about how far I'd come. I took in the moment instead. It was spectacular.

The personal, emotional stuff came later. First were the roars.

Uruguay's delegation preceded ours. The applause for them from the hundred thousand fans in the stadium was polite and welcoming, but was no preparation for what greeted us when we marched through the tunnel and into this great roar cloud. It gave me chills I'd felt just once before, in 2011, when I carried our flag into Ohio Stadium. It takes a while for 555 people to enter an already jammed stadium. The applause was relentless. This is what I thought then:

We're on a different continent, with a stadium full of people who don't speak our language. These people aren't cheering us. They're cheering an ideal. Our ideal.

In that moment, I understood what the United States meant to the rest of the world. To feel that welcome because we represent something bigger than ourselves, and to know I was part of it, right here and right now, that's what I took from the Opening Ceremony. That's what I'll remember.

I summoned the memory of my father, too. I always do. He'd have loved that moment. His pride would have been endless. *Damn, Ebs. Look at you.* If only.

My mom came to Rio and rented a bulletproof car. The stories back home about safety in Rio were exaggerated, even if the conditions in Rio weren't great. The men's basketball team slept on a cruise ship for a couple weeks. The rest of us bunked on what amounted to cots. We had bottled water to drink and to pour on our toothbrushes. To protect ourselves from the Zika virus, we drowned ourselves in repellent lotion. Each room also had a plug-in repellent sprayer.

This was no big deal to me. I'd been in worse places. It mainly served to remind me how lucky I was to live in America. Travel's greatest gift is perspective.

We had four days before we played our first match, against Argentina. Twelve countries in three pools would compete. The top two teams from each pool would advance to the medal round, along with the next two sides with the best point differentials.

Our pool comprised Argentina, Fiji, Brazil, and us. Brazil didn't qualify but made the field as the host team. Fiji was the reigning world Sevens champion. We thought we'd win easily over Brazil and keep it close against Fiji. Our hopes for the medal round came down to how we'd do against Argentina.

Back in Foxboro, Massachusetts, Bill Belichick stopped Patriots practice and put the match on in the team meeting room at Gillette Stadium. The day before, Matthew Slater wore my jersey, number 43, at practice. On this day, every player was wearing number 12, in my honor. That's because in Fifteens rugby, all the positions are numbered. The center, my position, wears number 12. My dad wore number 12 when he played Fifteens. Sevens carries no such distinction, but I appreciated the sentiment. Patriots fans assumed it was a tribute to another, higher profile number 12, Tom Brady.

It was the biggest rugby match of my life. I was as calm as I could be. I've been in enough big moments to know not to psych myself out. I've prepared for it, I've learned that nervous energy is wasted energy. I'm best when I'm in Fuck It mode, living the moment, not obsessing over it.

We came in prepared and confident. We'd finished ahead of the Argentines in the Sevens World Series and beaten them head-to-head more than they'd beaten us. We had the elite speed and finishers to counter Argentina's deliberately sloppy and brutish style. We felt ready for a moment that had been ninety-two years in the making.

And yet something wasn't right. It was as simple to diagnose as it was complicated to fix, and we definitely couldn't fix it in the moment.

We were tired.

There is an art to entering a major competition at your physical best. You don't want to undertrain before competing. You lose your edge that way. You don't want to overdo it, either. No one chooses to leave his best effort on a practice field. It's the finest of balancing acts that gets you to peak at the right time.

It's easy in hindsight to say we weren't at our physical best against Argentina. We did not want to come to the Olympics undertrained. With that in mind, did we overdo it in camp? That's hard for me to say. It was a factor. How big? Not nearly as big as the numerous chances we missed to win the game. But I'd be lying if I said we didn't break training camp wondering if we'd peaked physically a little early.

The game kicked off at noon in brutal heat. Cloudless sky, sun directly overhead. When I run onto a field before any game,

I want my energy level to be peaking. I want to feel electric, literally, as if a current is running through me. I want to explode with energy.

That didn't happen against Argentina. We ran from the tunnel to the field, and a heat-induced haze gripped our whole team.

It didn't help that we were playing Argentina. Every team has its style. New Zealand's All Blacks, for example, are simply a well-oiled machine. They play their game, make you play it, and it's usually good enough. The US game is about movement and flow, good tackling and precise passing. The Argentines are bare-knuckle. They want you to tackle them. The Argentines love the dirt.

It's an exhausting way to play. If you don't want to fight at every ruck or run to make every tackle, the Argentines will out-will you. That's what they did to us in the first half of a game we knew we had to win to have any chance of making the medal round.

The kickoff was a sign of what was to come. Danny Barrett made a fantastic play to keep the ball in bounds and win the ball for us, then not more than five seconds later, we lost it with a careless knock-on. We dropped a simple pass and the ball bounced forward.

From that point on, it was all Argentina in the first half and the start of the second half. We never got into our systems. We never spread their defense and attacked the gaps in their line. In fact, we barely had the ball, maybe a minute total in the first half. We played Argentina's game. We made mistakes that even included a couple "seal-off" penalties. When your ballcarrier is tackled, you can't just dive on top of him to seal the ball off from the other team's players. We knew that. Everyone who plays rugby knows that. We did it anyway.

Argentina scored with 3:30 to play in the half, when their ballcarrier literally ran over Madison Hughes on his way to scoring a try. Madison is normally a very sure tackler. It was an apt metaphor for how we were playing. Slowly, almost passively. And yet, we trailed just 7–0 at halftime.

That changed early in the second half. Argentina scored a try that should have been ruled a knock-on. As their ballcarrier approached the in-goal (goal line). Garrett Bender hit him, then Danny Barrett tackled him. The ball squirted free and briefly rolled forward in the try zone before the Argentine grabbed it. That's a knock-on.

It was clear from the replay that the ball came out before the Argentine runner touched it down. The whole stadium saw it. He never grounded the ball with control. That's the definition of scoring a try. The referees even sent the play to the TMO (television match official) to be reviewed. He called the evidence inconclusive and awarded the try. Argentina led, 12–0 with five minutes left.

I made my Olympic debut then. I hadn't started the match. Maka Unufe had, which was OK by me. He'd been a member of the national team before my arrival. He deserved it. As our center, my job on offense was to get the ball to Perry Baker in space. That meant attacking the space between my defender and the wing, where Perry operated. If my defender left me to mark Perry, the space was mine. Otherwise, I'd try to draw Perry's guy toward me, then get the ball to Perry. I'd be setting up tries and hopefully scoring a few. I had to be quick, smart, explosive, and strong. Find the space, exploit it. Centers are usually the best tacklers, too. Tackling wasn't a problem for me.

That day, I had another more immediate task: bring some energy to the game. We were down but not desperate. Four-plus minutes is a long time in a fourteen-minute, nonstop game. Zack Test and I entered the match with 4:30 to play. I like to think we brought some life with us.

One of Zack's first Olympic experiences was to be tackled and dumped on his head. That was a penalty and gave us the ball in a lineout. Zack caught a pass off the lineout. His first option was to pass the ball from where he was, on the left side of our line, to me in the middle of the field. Argentina's defenders were sliding toward Zack, and I ran a hard line, coming in from the right, against the flow. I was so open, I'd have needed only to break one arm tackle to sprint down the sideline and score. Zack kept the ball instead. It wasn't a bad decision, but it was almost costly.

Zack broke the Argentine line and sprinted for the corner. Perry Baker and I were flying down the field, practically in Zack's footsteps. I was so close, I inadvertently kept a guy from getting to Zack to make the tackle. That's an obstruction penalty and Argentina's ball. The refs didn't call it. Zack raced down the sideline but was tackled a foot from the Argentine in-goal.

He knocked it on, too, fumbling the ball forward as he hit the ground. Another potential disaster, but the refs called a high tackle on the Argentine defender and decided that the tackle kept Zack from scoring the try. Madison Hughes made the penalty try and the conversion. We dodged two bullets in one phase. We were right back in the game, down 12–7 with 3:26 to play.

Finally, we were playing our game, maintaining possession of the ball, running and stretching Argentina, cleaning up their messy style. Playing defense is not what you want to do in Sevens, especially not against a team like ours, which is good at making you chase. We had them tired and a little disorganized. It paid off when Danny Barrett took a pass from five meters out and, in vintage Beast fashion, deliberately changed his course to run over an opponent and into the try zone. Hughes's conversion put us ahead 14–12. It looked as if we would survive Argentina—and ourselves. We kicked off with forty-six seconds to play. I'll remember those forty-six seconds the rest of my life.

All we had to do was stop them to win and very likely ascend to the medal round. We couldn't find a way to do that. As Mike Friday said at the time, "It came down to moments. Most Sevens matches do."

There were any number of moments in those last forty-six seconds when we could have ended the game. We didn't get any of them right. That's what breaks my heart.

Our restart (kickoff) didn't go the required ten meters. "Not ten" in rugby parlance. That's a turnover, a huge mistake, and it gave Argentina a chance it shouldn't have had. Ironically, kickoffs were a strength of our game in 2016. Think of every kickoff as an NFL onside kick. We were very good at popping the kick high in the air, giving one of our speed guys on the wing a chance to run underneath it. We'd been the best team that year in the Sevens Series at retaining our kickoffs.

On this crucial kick, Perry and I lined up to the kicker's right. We'd be his first option. But Argentina so respected our speed, they marked me with two players on the outside and slid their two players guarding the center of the field noticeably toward Perry. That left them three players to cover the rest of the line. Seeing that, we decided to kick away from the double-team. The kickoff went seven or eight meters and out of bounds. My dad would have called that a mortal sin. Argentina took over at the fifty-meter (midfield) line.

Time was not a factor; rugby matches don't end when the time on the clock runs out. They're over when a possession ends.

The Argentines had the ball, we were chasing them. The first team to make a mistake would lose. We made a fatal mistake. We left the system on defense. The clock showed all zeroes when one of our guys strayed from the line to try to make a play on his own. He anticipated a pass that didn't happen. That created a gap in the middle of our line. Argentina took advantage immediately. The ballcarrier faked the pass, then ran through the hole in our line, before making the next pass in the telling final sequence.

Unless you're 100 percent sure you can finish the play, leaving the system is not a good move. It messes up the shape of the line. You simply cannot be out of position—shape—in Sevens. I ran from the wing to the middle of the field to plug the hole and keep the integrity of our shape. The Argentinians are not elite passers. One of their passes actually came up short, hit the ground, and . . . bounced straight back up and into the hands of one of their players.

A rugby ball isn't round, it's oblong, like a fat football. It's supposed to take wayward hops. Not that time. Their guy caught it and passed quickly to the outside. What we saw next looked like the end of our medal aspirations: a receiver catching the pass at the twenty-two-meter line and not a defender in sight. Our line was bunched in the middle. The ballcarrier sprinted to our right corner. I was the closest American to him, and I wasn't within five meters of the guy when he crossed the in-goal.

It's amazing how many turns a game lasting just fourteen minutes can take. We played poorly for two-thirds of the match, rallied for three minutes, then lost it all in the last forty-six seconds.

Maybe we were tight. You can't play any sport that way. You really can't play Sevens rugby nervous and hesitant. It messes with your rhythm and flow. It wasn't as if we didn't have our chances, especially in the second half. Argentina even had three yellow cards, two after halftime. A yellow card takes a player out of the match for two minutes. For six of the fourteen minutes, we had at least a one-player advantage.

At one point late in the game, Argentina had two guys sitting with yellow cards. We had a seven-on-five advantage and still couldn't pull out the win.

Our finishers Perry Baker and Carlin Isles were our strengths, but we didn't play to them. As for me, I wasn't thinking about realizing my dream. I was thinking about my energy level. All the moments in those last forty-six seconds—the kickoff, the freelancing on defense, the perfect bounce, the gap in the line—and we lost them all. We even had two chances in rucks in those final seconds. The team with the ball usually keeps it in a ruck, but it's still one of the best chances to force a turnover. Argentina worked hard at every breakdown so we couldn't counterruck and steal the ball.

The pregame fears that we'd overtrained were realized. "Some of us were overcooked," Danny Barrett said.

During World War II, US Army general George S. Patton wrote in a letter to his troops, "Fatigue makes cowards of us all." What most people don't remember is the rest of his quote: "Men in condition do not tire."

Fatigue happens when your body is pushed past the limits of preparation. We were used to that. Yaka Yards defined that. It was the little moments that killed us. Were they because we were tired? I don't know. Even if I did, I'd never use that excuse. In big, competitive situations, you don't get to make mistakes. Whether it's the Olympics or the NFL postseason, you don't get to play poorly for two-thirds of the game and still win it.

The little moments versus Argentina (and again versus Fiji) would most inform Mike Friday and the team in the years after Rio. They would lead to more mental training, more practicing of situations. A bit less conditioning. The best thing to come from the loss to Argentina—the only good thing—is what we were able to learn from it.

We couldn't dwell on it, though. Four hours later, we played Brazil.

"We knew how important that game was," Madison Hughes said. "We were (ranked) sixth in the world. They were seventh. That win would set us up to get out of pool play. To lose the way we did . . ."

I thought after that we had to beat Brazil and Fiji to advance to the medal round. Beating Brazil wasn't difficult, but we also had to run up the score to do it, to increase our points differential.

We won 26–0. Scoring twenty-six points in a fourteen-minute match is impressive but, as it turned out, not enough. I scored early, even got a yellow card for a penalty. "Good to see the NFL in him come out," Danny Barrett joked later. Brazil was moving the ball laterally toward the sideline and the guy with the ball kept dummy (fake) passing, trying to get Carlin to bite. Carlin was our last guy on the line. I was coming across as Carlin was giving ground.

The guy kept on with the dummy passes, so I lined him up and went what we call "full send" on him. As I committed to my hit he let go of the ball. You could say I was slightly late. I hit him hard and kind of high. He flopped on the ground and didn't get up, so the ref carded me. So it goes. We needed to set a tone.

As things turned out, if we'd scored five more points against Brazil—one more try—we'd have advanced to the medal round.

We didn't know that before we played Fiji, obviously. We only knew we needed to win.

That was a big ask against Fiji. The Fijians always have big, physical players, some of whom defy logic. How else do you explain speed guys who are six feet, five inches tall? That said, they don't like to play us. We can be just as physical, and with Carlin and Perry the US Sevens has tremendous speed on the wings. When we play good defense and tackle well, our speed is hard for them to handle.

The game went back and forth. I scored a try late in the match to pull us to within five, 24–19. We missed the conversion (two points), though, and that would be crucial. We had one last chance, but we messed up our own lineout and lost the ball. Game over. Another little moment, lost.

In rugby, a lineout is a set piece to restart the game when the ball goes "into touch," that is, out of bounds. One player throws the ball in from the sideline to a "jumper," who is hoisted by two mates on their side of the imaginary "tunnel." The team throwing it in knows where the ball will be thrown, short or long, fast or slow.

The jumper catches the ball in the air then quickly passes it to a teammate. Against Fiji, the play was supposed to go like this:

Folau Niua throws in from the sideline to the jumper Zack Test, lifted by Danny Barrett and Ben Pinkelman. Zack catches, then throws off the top, back to Folau, who has come around from the sideline. Folau passes to Madison Hughes, who passes to me. I put Carlin away on the wing and let his speed decide things.

But we didn't get the ball off the top. Fiji sacked the lineout and turned us over. And that was that.

Another crucial, last-second mistake. As it was, we needed to win that game or lose by four points or fewer to advance from pool play. We lost by five, 24–19. New Zealand edged us out for the medal round. Fiji eventually won the gold medal. Argentina finished fourth. Actually, the Argentines lost in overtime to Britain, who then got smoked by Fiji in the final. The final easily could have been two teams from our pool.

"We needed to be as close to perfect as possible," Danny Barrett would say later. "We weren't."

Winning and losing assume a suddenness in big games and at big events. You can spend months, sometimes years, preparing for one instant, and when that instant arrives, how you deal with it becomes part of you forever.

The US ended up ninth—the best we could finish after being knocked out of the medal rounds—after beating Brazil again, and Spain. If we'd handled our business versus Argentina, not messed up the lineout against Fiji and made a few soft tackles, also against Fiji, we'd have been in the running for a medal. Americans might not know that rugby is Fiji's national sport, or that the Fijians are world-class rugby players. Americans do know medals.

Winning a medal in Rio would have meant exposure for rugby in America. Exposure is another word for money. The rest of the world thought we met or exceeded expectations at those Olympics. Of course, the rest of the world didn't think we'd even qualify. We saw it as a huge disappointment and an opportunity lost. It showed us only what we needed to do to complete our gold-medal mission in Tokyo in what we assumed would be 2020.

Not long after the Olympics, I wrote Mike Friday a long letter. We both understood how close we'd come to glory and how far we still had to go. In the letter, I leaned on my Patriots experience, which by August of that year I thought would resonate with Mike. When I'd gotten to Chula Vista in March, he knew next to nothing about Bill Belichick, Tom Brady, and the dynasty growing in New England. We talked about it during the run-up to Rio. He was intrigued.

In the letter, I mentioned how the Patriots are always seeking an edge. Training, conditioning, one more film session, one new scheme to rush the punter. Anything that might make them better prepared than the next team they were playing. It's a league designed for every team to go 8–8, I told Friday. How do the Pats defy that intention every year?

I tied it in with the need for us to play more situational rugby. One mistake kept us out of the medal round: the restart kick that didn't travel the required ten meters, in our opening-round match against Argentina. We turned the ball over with no time left on the clock, the Argentines scored, and one match into our Olympic run, we were in a giant hole.

That was the moment that defined our Olympics. We should never have put ourselves in that moment.

In football, everything is situational. Second down and long, third and short, the red zone, fourth and one. The Patriots coach to every situation. Rugby's flow doesn't allow for nearly as much hands-on, situational coaching. But it does allow for some. The restart would have been one.

Your team is leading and kicking off with no time left on the clock. The game ends with the next play stoppage. What do you do? Kick the ball deep and inbounds, at such an angle that the ball is likely to bounce out of bounds. Game over.

Kick the ball ten meters, win the ball, kick it out of bounds. Game over.

At the very least, kick the ball deep and in play and make the opponent go ninety meters for the winning try. We can talk all day about the kick that didn't go ten meters. We need to talk more about the strategies we can use to avoid that situation.

My letter made an impression on Friday, enough that he wanted to see for himself how the Patriots' culture worked. In the spring of 2017, he came to Foxboro for a few days to watch Organized Team Activities. He left with a better understanding and appreciation for how our culture was important to our success. And how our unselfishness and work ethic could be applied to his own ideas of team building.

A few years later on British television, Friday discussed his experiences in Foxboro. "Belichick is process driven," he said.

"When he addresses the team, you're under no illusion where you stand. He is very much that detached figurehead. Analytical. No emotion.

"They train for two hours, it's like military. Then they come back in and review everything. These boys are all business on the pitch and in the classroom. It's a long day. Seven (a.m.) to seven (p.m.). Seven to nine if you're a rookie. If you don't do it, you're gone."

Our Rio experience also showed Friday we weren't as together as we needed to be. There is a fundamental dependence on one another in Sevens. Anything we can do to get to know one another better is important.

Since 2016 Friday has worked hard on this. "I had to get them thinking about each other, how they related. The openness needed, the vulnerability expressed," he explained not long ago. He'd actually wanted to incorporate some of this during the pre-Olympic camp, but decided physical conditioning was more important. (Ironically, by the time we got to Rio, the consensus among the players was that we'd overtrained. Danny Barrett didn't even play the second half of the Fiji match and conceded it was because he was gassed.)

"Not everyone thinks the way you do. The trick is overlooking that and overcoming it. It's essential to Sevens because we are so interdependent on the field, we have to understand how each of us ticks," Friday said.

In-game coaching isn't a big factor in Sevens. The speed and the absence of time-outs make players coaches on the field. The trust has to be there, and it can't disappear when a mistake is made.

The team takes classes in this stuff now. It has for three years. It might seem ironic to the uninitiated. Tough guys talking about "feelings" and "relating." But in a game of suddenness, there is no pausing to pout. As Danny Barrett put it recently, "We communicate so easily now, we're all just making sounds."

"We're learning not to get frustrated with each other," was how Ben Pinkelman described it. "Mistakes are part of the game. Shake them off, keep your heads, get back in the game."

Since 2016 the national Sevens team has been an impressive work in progress, with about two-thirds of the same players still on the team. They finished second in the World Series in 2018–19. Optimism is realistic for Tokyo, even as the competition has been delayed a year. That doesn't change what went down in Rio.

"The ball is shaped funny," Danny Barrett said. "It's gonna bounce funny. One bounce could change the score." I didn't really believe that until the Argentines converted that perfect bounce into the try that beat us.

The day after our last match in Rio, I was on a plane to Boston, to rejoin Patriots' training camp.

TWENTY-TWO

Validation

I'm not sure I can top 2016. I certainly don't dwell on it. What's done is done, what's next is what matters. I was an NFL player who performed in the Olympics, became an All-Pro, and won a Super Bowl ring in one eleven-month span. Could I come close to doing that again? Never say never.

It's hard to describe the satisfaction in devoting a decade of your life to believing in that one true thing, then seeing that devotion emerge, authentic and honored, in real time. I can't express that. I can only feel it: giving everything I have, being uncomfortable during the process, pushing past my limits, then coming out the other side exhilarated and confident. Knowing that achievement is part of me forever. Nothing makes me feel more alive.

It's so easy to lay out and so difficult to pull off. Believe in the process. Commit to it. Don't deviate. Let the results speak for you. With success comes confidence, with confidence comes success. The whole thing builds on itself. What I'm about, what I can do when I give everything, when I empty the toolbox of all my dad's lessons. Validation, confirmation, affirmation. Whatever you call it. That's the story of my life. Nothing matched that.

Not the Opening Ceremony or the tries I scored or how close we came to reaching the medal round. Being an Olympian was good. Being the only active NFL player ever to be an Olympian—then returning to the NFL to win a Super Bowl—was better. Seeing my dad's process succeed at two of the most spectacular events in sports was the highlight. Making that 2016 team in Rio was a tribute to my copilot who watched from somewhere, as I flew solo.

It was a love letter penned in sweat, to a sport I never gave up on. Personal validation is its own reward. It's tied to things I can control. The process of making the Olympics was strictly personal. So was the reward. How the team did depended on all of us.

You can do everything you can to prepare for a moment, and owning that moment still isn't guaranteed. There was no Olympic medal around my neck. We'd missed the medal round because we made a few minor mistakes. A big opportunity went begging in Rio.

I rode the Olympic wave into the NFL season. I was moving well, I was in good shape. I kept the Fuck It I'd found in Tours the previous spring, when my Olympic chances were on the ropes. Fearless and smart is a good way to play special teams. I had both in 2016. I just went out and balled.

I led the league in special teams tackles and made All-Pro for the only time in my career. And then we beat Atlanta in the Super Bowl, on February 5, 2017, in the greatest comeback in Super Bowl history.

Two years later, I earned ring number three. We started the 2018 season riding a crest of doubting questions: Is Tom too old? Can Bill stay a step ahead of the rest of the league?

It didn't help we started 1–2, with bad road losses at Jacksonville and Detroit. Tom Brady was forty-one years old. Belichick had been grinding as a head coach for twenty-four seasons. The skepticism wasn't new. Predicting our demise had been popular before 2018.

This stuff doesn't bother me, until it does. I try to ignore the negative noise from those who don't play the game or understand it. It affects my chi, and not in a good way. That said, I did get fed up hearing about "the decline of the Patriots," and I did use it as motivation. And when the year ended in my third ring ceremony, I was heavily satisfied.

I'd also come back from a torn ACL suffered at Miami the previous November. Typically, that injury mandates an eight- to twelve-month rehab. I got back in eight months (too soon, probably) and played in fifteen games. I was fully healthy for one game all year. I endured. Again, satisfaction.

The Super Bowl itself? The Los Angeles Rams came in

riding high, going 13–3 in the regular season while scoring the second-most points in the league. They had a young quarterback, twenty-four-year-old Jared Goff, tutored by a young coach and budding offensive mastermind, thirty-three-year-old Sean McVay, and running back Todd Gurley, who'd scored twenty-one touchdowns.

We had "aging" Tom Brady and, statistically, an average defense that ranked twentieth of thirty-two teams in yards allowed. And we had old-guy Belichick, who of course was getting worn down by the grind of excellence.

We won, 13–3.

Our defense completely confused McVay and Goff. We were clinical in our ability to disguise our defenses, to the extent it seemed as if we would call two distinct defenses on each play. We gave a twenty-four-year-old quarterback playing in his first Super Bowl a lot to think about. Jared Goff completed only half his passes and threw a crucial interception with seven minutes left in the game. Gurley ran for thirty-five yards.

I heard McVay say he "got outcoached," to the surprise of no one who knew our way of doing things.

Our special teams ate up the hidden yards. The Rams had twelve possessions. Three times, they started inside their 10-yard line. Nine times, they began at their 28 or worse.

We'd won three Super Bowls in five years. That's almost impossible in a league of enforced parity, where the best teams get the hardest schedules and the lowest draft picks, and every team has the same cash pile to spend on players. That's a system designed to produce the more perfect 8–8 record. The New England Patriots haven't been worse than 9–7 since 2000.

It's an achievement I'll never lose. I guess that's why I like the ring ceremony so much. There's no BS, no fraudulence, just the celebration of knowing you've reached the mountaintop where few others will stand. That Super Bowl ring is a piece of forever, man.

GIVING IT A GO in Tokyo in 2021 is still a possibility. The variables shift. The conditions change, depending on my health and my status in the NFL. I'd like to play football for two more years at least. A decade in the NFL is a nice achievement. Would I want to risk that by playing rugby in Tokyo?

The motivation would be different a second time around. Rio de Janeiro was for my dad, my family, and my love of the game. Playing in Rio was the finish line for a trip I'd been on since that first tackle with Scioto Valley.

Playing in Tokyo would be for me. I'd play simply because I couldn't say no. I'd play for no other reason than because I wanted to. It wouldn't be about validation. Been there, done that. If someone doubts me after what I've accomplished, I couldn't care less because I know what I've done and the work I've put in to get there, and no one can change that or take it from me. I am validated.

My dad loved to say "rest when you die." If I'm still able and capable—healthy and good enough—there's a solid chance I'll re-up for the pain of training camp. If I can, then I must. My obsessiveness kicks in again. If I don't do it, somebody else will, so why not me? I'll rest when I die.

A 2021 run would be different from the one in 2016. I'd know what to expect, and what would be expected of me. The naysayers likely would be replaced by people assuming I'd make the team. I wouldn't be an underdog. That's unfamiliar turf for me.

We have unfinished business in Japan, and an unmatched opportunity. We had a good team in Rio. This team, by all accounts, is better. As Danny Barrett put it, "If we kept the Rio 12 and took them all to Tokyo, we'd be unstoppable."

It's the same group that just finished second in the Sevens series. But it's a fragile success. New Zealand, England, Australia, and South Africa still have better financial support. After USA Rugby filed for bankruptcy in March 2020, rugby in America was on shaky financial ground, even as the National Sevens team escaped most of the consequences. What Fiji lacks in money it owns in national passion and prestige.

America's best chance is right now. Our core players are generational talents. They're that good and experienced. They've learned and grown from the mistakes of 2016. They're also getting older. No one knows if the players coming up will be better, or even as good.

I'd go into the 2021 Games on better footing. I'd know the players, I'd be familiar with the style Mike Friday wants to play. The conditioning grind wouldn't be a surprise. The Fuck It that I lacked for months last time will be there from the start. Four years is a long time, though, and in some ways we'd all be starting from scratch. I haven't been around the team since Rio. The competition will probably be better.

Sevens is a young man's game. The definition of "young" in pro sports is not the same for me as for you. I'm thirty-one as I write this in early 2020. That is old in Sevens, unless you're Folau Niua, whose age nobody really knows, but who is at least thirty-four. I'd have to be better in 2021 than I was in 2016.

Can I find the Why? I've had a strong Why for a long time. My dad was my Why in college. Keeping my promise to him was my Why in the NFL. I satisfied the Olympic Why in 2016. Now?

Friday offered this evaluation in May 2019: "I'd give him a chance. He'd be four years older and four years removed from playing with the core. We've matured a lot since then. But Nate's ability to focus on what he wants will always give him a chance."

He knows me well. I'd get my chance. I've never needed more.

Meantime, Steve Tomasin told me about a new torture drill they're doing. "The Bronco" is twenty meters and back, forty and back, sixty and back. Five times, sprinting.

Oh, man.

TWENTY-THREE

Where We Go
from Here

In 2008, I made a life-changing choice to walk away from love.
It wasn't that hard.

Passion works when it comes with a future. I had no professional future in rugby. I'd taken it as far as I could. I didn't want
to move overseas to earn a decent living. I respect every teammate I've ever had for hanging with the rugby dream as it exists
in our country. It wasn't for me. With no regrets, I set aside
rugby for college football and a shot at the NFL. More than a
decade later, not much has changed.

Rugby in the US still relies more on love than money. We've
recently been able to use the carrot of the Olympics to find and
retain elite players, asking even the best of them to live paycheck

to paycheck. Before that, we could offer our best players only a chance to see the world.

"We have the best athletes in the world," said Al Caravelli, the men's national Sevens team coach between 2006 and 2012. We don't support them financially the way our closest competitors do. I wonder what we could do with New Zealand's budget. Or England's, or South Africa's.

Other countries with teams in the Series get by with fewer resources than we do. Kenya, for example. But if we aspire to have a top-tier program, the players need to be paid that way.

"We're the NFL of the 1950s," Caravelli said. "They're making a living, but they still need side jobs and sponsorships. It's a chicken-and-egg thing. You have to win before you get paid." And, it must be said, it helps to be solvent.

Salary figures aren't public. A November 2017 story in the online magazine *Rugby Today* claimed that the best Sevens players make $24,000 a year. That number has gone up significantly since. Players are paid performance bonuses if the team does well in Sevens Series events. The US won two Series tournaments in the 2018–2019 season and finished second overall in the Series. Players moonlight doing camps and a few have sponsorships. Yet none makes even $50,000 a year.

Let's do some math. The average monthly rent for a two-bedroom apartment in San Diego in December 2019 was $2,286. Let's suppose that before taxes, the average salary of a Sevens player is $30,000. After taxes, that's close to $24,000. If the apartment rent is split with another player, it's $1,143 a month. Multiplied by 12 months, that's $13,716, or 46 percent of a year's net salary. And we're not even talking about car expenses. In San Diego, you better have a vehicle. Even if it's just to get to and from the training center.

It's discouraging that the sport I love has not made more progress in paying its players a living wage. If only the salaries reflected the progress the Men's Sevens program has made.

It's important to remember that America is still new to Sevens rugby. The US wasn't even a member of the Sevens "core" circuit—among the top twelve sides in the world, competing in the World Cup Series—until 2008. We weren't expected to qualify for the '16 Olympics. We finished ninth. Our progress has continued since.

We've come a long way from my first national Sevens team training camp at the US Military Academy in 2006. At West Point, the team stayed in barracks without hot water. That's one way to get the blood pumping early in the morning.

Caravelli turned around our national Sevens program, beginning with his 2006 hiring. He spent the next six years hustling, begging, and growing the sport.

Caravelli guided Sevens from amateur to professional status. He raised $75,000 his first year. USA Rugby matched it. He scoured America's Division I colleges, looking for athletes. They didn't have to be rugby players. Caravelli could teach them the game. He couldn't teach them how to be fast, have good footwork, and be exceptionally coordinated. Work ethic was not something he could script on a dry-erase board.

He looked at football players, soccer players, and water polo players and saw rugby players. He was able to get good-paying jobs overseas for his best players, with the caveat he could call them home when he needed to. That was a temporary solution to the players' money problems. Teams paying Caravelli's guys upwards of $150,000 wanted more control over them.

Caravelli had to fight the perception that Sevens rugby was something the Fifteens players did in the off-season to stay in shape. He had to fight the notion, rampant even among his own players, that no one expected them to succeed. "The mentality was, we're amateurs, nobody expects us to win," Caravelli once explained. "We're happy just wearing the jersey.

"But professionalism isn't about how much you get paid," Caravelli went on. "It's an attitude, and a commitment you make. If I have to turn over the entire team, I will." Even knowing his players had full-time jobs, Caravelli expected them to work out two hours in the morning and two hours at night. "I expect you to come to camp fit," he told them.

Early on, Caravelli asked one of his best players, Chris Wyles, what mattered to him.

"Respect," Wyles answered. "No one respects us. We're everyone's doormat." For example, Wyles told Caravelli, "We like to trade jerseys. No one wants our jersey."

By 2008, with a big assist from Wyles, the US Sevens were

competing with the likes of England, Fiji, and Samoa. Al Caravelli was a workaholic. When he wasn't coaching, he was recruiting. When he wasn't recruiting, he was trying to raise money.
He'd get to major rugby events by asking tournament directors
to pay for his flight. Their compensation would be in the exposure
players would get from auditioning for the national Sevens coach.
Then Caravelli would bunk at a friend's house for the duration.

He flew to Oregon to meet with Nike officials to fill his
team's kits with gear. He worked seven days a week and slept
four hours a night until he resigned in 2012. Caravelli has seen
the progress we've made since and says it's not good enough.

"We need attendance and viewership," he said in 2019. In
2012, USA Rugby asked Caravelli to stay on as full-time coach of
the national Sevens. It offered to pay him $45,000. He turned it
down. He was tired from the barnstorming. Plus, he noted, "I
have a son going to Cal. His tuition is more than that."

Alex Magleby inherited the team from Caravelli. In his two
years as coach, Magleby installed a style of rugby that took the
US team to its highest-ever finishes on the circuit to that point.
Mike Friday has built steadily on the foundation laid by Mags
and Caravelli. The success of the Sevens program has been remarkable, given the financial challenges we've faced. Friday is
the head coach. He's also the point man for the growth of Sevens
in the US. He talked about that in January 2020, on a rugby-
themed British talk show, *House of Rugby*:

"Coaching the rugby on the pitch is the easy bit. I've got great
people around me. Trying to create the pathways, the platform,

and the program in a ridiculously big country on a budget that isn't near what they put in the grassroots game" in Great Britain can be a struggle.

Mike praised the Golden Eagles, the charitable organization founded by rugby players and fans in 2013 to support the USA Sevens team financially. But he acknowledged philanthropy alone won't work. Being "commercially viable is the key."

He and I agree that rugby has to grow at the high school level and that "a massive investment in the club game" is important, too. The potential is huge, Mike said, because of the size of the US and the number of "ridiculously" talented athletes here. "The states are so big, you just need to hit the rugby hotbeds. Six or seven states." Mike mentioned Utah, Massachusetts, Texas, Colorado, and California. "The best players will gravitate toward those states," he said.

His theory was that rugby will never replace football and basketball, because the best athletes will chase college scholarships—and the potential of pro careers—in those sports. The 99 percent who don't make the NBA or NFL might then consider the soft landing of rugby. "We've got a journey, similar to what happened to [Sevens]" in 1995, four years before the Sevens Series began.

Looked at that way, maybe we're right on schedule.

And then the world changed.

One thing I've learned as a professional athlete is to assume nothing. I've never played as if I've had it made. Football is a ruthless, fragile career. I can tear a knee or take one too many shots to the head. Even if I manage to stay healthy, eventually I'm going to be the old guy. There will always be younger, cheaper players. All I can control is my attitude.

My attitude was no match for the novel coronavirus. Nor could it overcome the financial disaster that USA Rugby had become, bad enough that the governing body of American rugby declared bankruptcy.

COVID-19 shut down rugby worldwide in March 2020. USA Rugby filed for bankruptcy in the same month. On March 24, 2020, Japan and the International Olympic Committee announced that the Tokyo Games would be postponed until July 2021.

I had just spent three weeks in March at the Olympic Training Center in Chula Vista, getting back into the rugby swing, when the virus forced the center to close. The good news for me was, the body felt good. The better news was I'd just signed a one-year deal as a free agent, to play for the New York Giants.

I wasn't looking to leave New England, but free agency gave me a chance to reassess my situation. Nothing lasts forever, especially in the NFL. I'd played for the Patriots for eight years, almost a lifetime by the league's Darwinian measure. I'd won three championships and played for Bill Belichick, maybe the best coach in league history. It was a great run, but I needed to do what was best for me. This time, moving on was best.

I'd be reuniting with the Giants' new head coach, Joe Judge, who had been a special teams coach with the Patriots during my entire time in New England. Joe knows my value to a team as much as anyone.

In truth, the one-year postponement of the Games very likely saved my rugby career, at least as a potential member of the Olympic team. When I signed with the Giants, I told Judge I'd be happy to help him establish the winning standards we'd both learned and experienced with the Pats under Belichick. That would mean staying in New York, not traveling with the national Sevens team as I'd done in the spring of 2016. It would make it impossible for me to attend Olympic training camp.

I'd come to terms with not having an Olympic chance in 2020. The way it is now, if everything works out, I'll have a small opportunity to give it a go in the spring of 2021. The door isn't completely shut.

Happily, the national Sevens players felt the same way. For them, the postponement was practically a blessing. A few key players were hurting. Ben Pinkelman had a bad back. Folau Niua had a terrible leg break in June 2019. As Pinkelman said, "This team would have been hobbling into the Olympics."

The team hadn't been playing as well as it should have been. They finished second in the World Cup series in 2018–19. The following year, they were in sixth place when coronavirus canceled the season. Injuries played into it, but so did the ongoing roster churn familiar to all sports.

The 2018–19 team was a veteran group that knew how to win the big moments and had developed a nice chemistry. The team the following year had good young players who needed "blooding," as Mike Friday put it. "Little errors at critical moments," he said. "You have to get it wrong to get it right." The extra year will give the young players time to learn on the job.

It doesn't come without a cost, though. Nothing does. Folau will be thirty-six in 2021. (At least we think he will be thirty-six. No one knows for sure.) His body needed the extra time to heal, but what will another year on that body take from his game?

Danny Barrett had planned to retire from rugby after Tokyo. He had a job lined up that was to begin in September 2020. He was getting married. "Start a family, get a real paycheck," he said. That was the new goal. Now he has to shift mental gears.

The one-year detour from real life doesn't bother Danny, even as he wonders how his thirty-one-year-old body will deal with it. "Playing a full season, to play in one tournament," he said. "Can I handle that, mentally and physically?"

Danny said the following in May 2020. He sounded like most of the older guys on the team:

"I get asked often, 'If you weren't playing sports, what would you be doing?' I say I don't want to do anything else. Rugby has given me so much. A college education, a trip to the Olympics. I'll never be able to repay the game."

Ben Pinkelman explained it this way: "We've been on this trek so long, it's been such a big part of our lives, one more year is not the end of the world. There's no rush to get to the rest of our lives."

The camaraderie that hooks you from the beginning keeps its hold on you until the end.

Steve Tomasin was waiting in the wings even before the 2016 Olympics in Rio. He barely missed making that team. Since then, he has been a star, ascendant. Two seasons ago, Stevie was a finalist for World Cup Sevens player of the year. Had the Tokyo Games been canceled, it would have devastated his career. "The last seven or eight years were all a buildup [to Tokyo] for me," he said. Now he just has to re-gear mentally. Physically, he'll be twenty-six. At his peak.

As it turned out, the US team had more than the pandemic to consider. While no one could have predicted COVID-19, but everyone in the rugby world could have foretold the bankruptcy declaration of USA Rugby. "Insurmountable financial constraints," the organization announced in March 2020.

USA Rugby has had money issues for a few years at least. It reported losses of $4 million in 2018. As recently as December 2019, USA Rugby needed a $1 million bailout from World Rugby—the world governing body for the sport—just to keep going. According to papers filed in bankruptcy court, USA Rugby's top creditor was World Rugby, to which it owed $3.6 million. The virus's closing down the sport merely hastened the bankruptcy proceedings.

In my opinion, USA Rugby's leadership has always been more concerned with making money than growing the game. They tried to sell the product before it was worth selling. USA Rugby invested in its marketing wing, Rugby International Marketing. It invested in the Rugby Channel, a subscription-based online streaming service, before Americans had developed a taste for the game. Both RIM and the Rugby Channel lost money.

USA Rugby put the cart before the horse. It needs to take a step back and shift its focus to governing our national teams and developing our youth programs, to create a product Americans might actually pay to watch.

As Mike Friday put it, "The game has to come first. Growing the game. Then, the national teams have to win. That trickles down to the local level. We need the game to get to where the kids want to be Danny Barrett and Madison Hughes."

The players on the National Sevens team weren't affected by the bankruptcy. The Golden Eagles, our fundraising arm, have always taken good care of us. This time was no different. Between the Golden Eagles and funding from the United States Olympic and Paralympic Committee, national Sevens players are getting paid.

"We are self-sufficient," Mike Friday declared in May 2020.

The same couldn't be said for Friday, whose salary was cut 50 percent, or his entire staff, which was either furloughed or let go. USA Rugby's offices in Colorado also eliminated positions.

It frustrates players. They see themselves sacrificing for the betterment of the game. They don't see equal concern coming from the top. Ben Pinkelman expressed it well: "Our goal is to help rugby the way rugby helped us. Without [management] able to hold itself accountable, what we do on the field isn't going to matter very much."

We can only hope that the restructuring will get the right people in place. Rugby has too much potential in the US for it to fail because of poor leadership.

The postponement of the 2020 Games didn't end a dream. It merely deferred it. In 2016, the US wasn't even expected to qualify for the Olympics. Approaching July 2021, we're considered a medal favorite. If a team that has only been in serious existence since 2006 can have a "golden era," our men's National Sevens team is living it now.

The core players have been together nearly a decade. Folau Niua, Danny Barrett, Madison Hughes, Martin Iosefo, Maka Unefe, Perry Baker, and Carlin Isles have the game and the experience to do great things in Tokyo. After that, nothing is guaranteed but advancing pages on the calendar. Barrett and Isles were thirty by August 2020. Baker was thirty-four. If you talk to current team members, they'll tell you the prospect of a gold medal is the biggest reason they've stuck around. Sevens is a young man's game mainly because you can't be thirty-five and stay in Sevens shape. But also because with age comes responsibility. You're not this pie-eyed twenty-one-year-old anymore, happy to have a few beers and a carton of eggs in the fridge at the end of the month. Life goes on and never gets less expensive. And as Friday put it on the British television show, "These boys live on the breadline. They'd earn just as much stacking the shelves at Walmart."

The financials tear at the players, because they love what they do and they know how lucky they are to do it. Madison Hughes is typical of the situation. He'll be twenty-eight when the Olympics are contested. Madison has played Sevens for the national team since 2014. He's the team captain.

"We make enough to get by," he said not long ago. "What could be better than traveling the world with great friends and playing rugby? Most of my friends are in investment banking and private equities, earning a shit-ton of money. And most are jealous of what I do."

Or as Danny Barrett put it, "As long as I'm playing a sport, I'm allowed to be as childish as I want. The day I stop playing is the day I stop having fun. Yaks are better than sitting behind a desk, punching keys on a computer." But Beast is sensitive to the realities of the situation.

"We're all in different parts of our lives. Do I want to keep coming back? Or do I want to start my life?"

I did both. I started my life, in a manner of speaking. I'm getting paid a lot of money to play a game. Nevertheless, I was able to do something different and still return to rugby. Not everyone is so fortunate.

Ben Pinkelman is twenty-seven and in his prime. He lives near the training center, which means he lives in the San Diego area, one of the most expensive places in the country. He spends half his take-home pay on rent. He eats for free at the center, but he's strapped for cash most of the time. An extravagance for him is an occasional night on the town.

Still, Ben says, "I'm playing a game for a living. I'm going to play as long as I can. I'll figure out the rest of my life when I have to." But he adds this: "The current wave can't continue without more financial support." USA Rugby's finances make that an open-ended proposition.

Perry Baker has two kids. Folau Niua is wearing down. All the core guys are, to some degree. Behind them, we have good young talent, but those guys aren't battle-tested. We don't have a developmental league. It's going to be more about rebuilding than reloading.

Mike Friday said this to *Rugby Today*, in September 2017:

"The USA is a Tier One economy, yet its [Sevens team] is resourced as a Tier Two/Three nation. The reality is that our players have to sacrifice and live below the minimum wage to represent their country."

This is why winning a medal in Tokyo is so important. Winning equals more viewers and participation and more sponsors. More attention overall, which means more money. Look at how women's soccer has boomed in the US since that team won its first Olympic gold medal in 1996.

I think Sevens rugby has a chance to earn its own significant spot on our sporting landscape. It's fast, it's violent (part of football's appeal, like it or not), the action never stops, and the people playing it are the kind of people you'd want to have a beer with. It could really use a shot of winning on the biggest international stage, at the Olympics. Americans might not understand rugby. They understand gold.

I'd like to be a part of the winning, if circumstances allow. We've come a long way in a relatively short time. Now's the time to take advantage. Having an additional year to prepare improves our chances.

TWENTY-FOUR

Something That
Requires Everything

I don't have an ultimate goal in life. That sounds like settling to me. The goals evolve, their shapes shift. Goals aren't part of the journey. They *are* the journey. Mine is far from over.

Making the football team at Ohio State wasn't an ultimate goal, it was a leaping-off point for my faith in myself. Was being an Olympian the ultimate? Was standing on the field two hours before my first Super Bowl? They sure seemed ultimate at the time. But why limit myself? I don't worry about finding meaning in my life after pro sports. There is so much ahead of me.

I want to be a father. I want to experience what my dad experienced in raising me. Approaching the success he had will be next to impossible, but I do like challenges. I'd love to feel some of what he felt, as he and I came to be coconspirators in plotting our remarkable journey together.

I want to repay Chelsey's years of patience for riding shotgun with my dreams. She has sacrificed some of who she is for me. I need to be around more, to do the same for her.

I don't think I want to coach football. I've donated enough hours to watching boring movies in windowless rooms. If you think playing in the NFL is life-consuming, try coaching in the NFL. The hours I'd put in, with my approach to working? No, thanks.

My temperament isn't exactly suited to coaching. It'd make me want to play. I'd get frustrated with guys who didn't see their jobs the way I saw mine. And I really couldn't picture myself as a college assistant. Could you see me, with my upbringing, trying to convince a pampered eighteen-year-old to come play football at State U? I'd be addicted to antinausea meds in a week.

There is a lure to the profession, though. Character can be taught and coached. I believe that. I saw Jim Tressel do it. "Molding young men" sounds corny. In worst-case scenarios, it sounds like a snake-oil coach covering bad deeds in righteous words. But it's real. At least it would be if I were doing the molding.

Youth rugby could be my path. I owe it to the sport to pay it forward. As an ambassador, maybe, appearing at youth clinics and tournaments. Come see the Olympian! I could talk up the game and encourage the kids to fall in love with it. I did. I turned out OK.

Growing the game has to start at the grass roots, on empty fields in anonymous towns, gathering a collection of interested kids and going from there. Once I got them to throw the ball around, that's all it would take.

They're luckier than I was. They have a professional model to admire. Major League Rugby started in 2018, a twelve-team testament to the growth of the sport in America. When I was a kid absorbing the game, my heroes were from New Zealand. If I wanted to watch matches, I had to search for them on the internet. These kids will see their heroes and idols at the punch of a remote button. They can relate in real time. They can aspire.

Major League Rugby is hardly an institution in the States. Maybe it never will be. But it's a start. Kids from a club in Wrentham, Massachusetts, can follow the MLR team in Boston. They can attend games. They can feel part of the team's success. Ideally, MLR gets big enough and televised enough, kids get hooked. Kids who are good athletes but not NFL prospects will see in rugby an outlet for their skills, and the prospect of making a little money. They'll go from MLR to the national teams, with the chance to make more money and benefit from international exposure. They'll have more options than I did.

The NFL wasn't an overnight sensation. In its infancy, the league filled its rosters with the same sort of players you'd see playing for Scioto Valley Rugby Club now. Tough guys in their off-hours, getting dirty on weekends.

I do think about what's next. I do wonder, like most pro athletes do, if anything could ever be better than what I've done already. Finding new meaning might be difficult after three Super Bowl rings.

I know only this: If I'm going to find new satisfaction, it will have to require as much of me as what I've done to this point. It will have to be something that requires everything.

I will wake up every day and say, "I gotta grind through this. I gotta find a way to make this work." Discovering who I am doesn't stop when the games end. I'm always going to look for new challenges deserving of my passion/obsession. New ways to find my Why.

Maybe at this point you're thinking, *Does this person ever free himself from challenges? It's a great, big world out there. Countries to visit, mountains to ski, beaches on which to do nothing. You've earned a new lifetime of doing nothing.*

Yeah, maybe.

I'll never do that.

Even if I tried, I'd always find things to be meticulous about, stuff to focus on. Grand plans and silly things. It's easy for me to think about renting a house for a month somewhere in the South Pacific, and still make sure all the dishes get put in the dishwasher. What is so hard, after you're done eating, to take your plate to the kitchen sink, scrub it well, and put it in the dishwasher?

My dad used to say "the dishwasher is not a power washer." Scrub the junk off, then put the dishes in the machine. Finish the job.

Anal? Or efficient? I can't just remove my work personality

like a three-piece suit, then put it back on when I need it. My personality has been bent to fit the challenges I've taken on.

I don't relax well. If I relax, I still need to be stimulated and focused. That's contradictory, I know, but I like to be submerged in whatever I'm doing, even if it's shooting pool or playing putt-putt golf. I don't want to play with you if you're goofing around. Playing for fun isn't fun. If I'm half-assing having fun, my mind will drift to things I should be doing. My perfect day has to leave me feeling I've accomplished something.

I can wear people out. I know this. It's always going to be about the process for me. My life is nothing if not a perpetual challenge, self-imposed. What am I able to overcome to get what I want and how much persistence and pain is required? How hard am I willing to work?

If I turn down those tests of self-discovery, I miss out. I know who I am today. I know who I've been. Who can I be tomorrow? We are what we do. Thinking and talking mean nothing.

I like to believe I'll get really obsessed with something. I'll find something worth losing myself in and submerging myself for, and I will grow from the process. The way I did on the road to Rio in 2016.

I know who I am: I'm a dog who wants to compete. I know why I'm good at it: I enjoy the exhausting journeys. The open road of What's Next doesn't worry me. I can't wait to rise up and meet it.

Epilogue

Chelsey and I want to have children soon. We're both on the back side of thirty, old enough to handle the responsibility, young enough to enjoy it fully. I've spent more than a decade keeping my promise to Jeff Ebner. Every day, I have tried to represent the influence he has had on me. It's an ongoing pledge. It's time to pay it forward.

I wonder what sort of father I will be. I don't know how to equate it with the rest of my life. Working hard and finishing strong: How do they translate to being a good dad? Parents can work too hard at being parents. Finishing strong means nothing if you don't start the same way.

Love and time. My mother and father gave me both. That was their promise to me, before and after they divorced. That was their unending gift. My life almost stopped when my dad died, but my mom wouldn't allow it. My dad formed my life. My mom saved it.

They worked together to make sure I was loved. My mother gave my dad more time with me than their divorce settlement provided. She knew he was a good parent. If they ever had issues, I never saw it. I had a healthy relationship with both of them, maybe because they had a healthy relationship with each other.

I look at what might have happened without that respect between my parents and I am humbled. National statistics, from both the US Census Bureau and various studies, show clearly that kids growing up in single-parent households suffer, sometimes terribly.

According to the US Census Bureau, approximately 30 percent of American families are headed by only one parent. That's twenty-four million kids in that situation. The US Department of Health says 63 percent of youth suicides are from fatherless homes. Ninety percent of runaways and homeless kids come from homes without dads. In 2002, a US Justice Department survey showed that 39 percent of incarcerated kids came from mother-only homes.

I think parenting is trial and error, mixing and matching until we're comfortable with the people we see in the family mirror. There is no one way to be great at parenting, but there are ageless ways to try. They start with love and time.

I will make the time for my children, because my dad did that for me. I remember the nearly nightly sight of his truck or his

Mercedes in the driveway of my mom's house, an hour from his own. And how that made me feel, which was priceless. To him I was priceless.

I will steal all the pages from his playbook (well, almost all). I might even use a little black book of my own. Except where my dad divided his into workout categories—rowing times and bench presses, mile runs and dead lifts—I might split mine into less measurable but equally important attributes. Character and respect, diligence and discipline.

Or maybe, I'll just remember how my dad did it, and the rest will fall in line.

I've been on this remarkably fulfilling journey my dad's parenting made possible, and he hasn't witnessed any of it. That makes me impossibly sad if I dwell on it. So I don't. The last Jeff Ebner knew of me, I was playing rugby at Ohio State and I had this seemingly crazy idea I could walk onto the football team and use it as a stepping-stone to a career in the NFL. That's all I know he knows.

If I had one wish, I'd want to sit down with him over a glass of Crown Royal and tell him how I've used the love and time he bestowed. We could reflect on my journey. That's all. I'd be curious what he'd ask me about.

I need to see things to believe them, I need proof to wrap my brain around. I can't relate to fantasies. Jeff Ebner might be floating around the stands, watching me play. Just as certainly, he might not be. The What Ifs don't interest me. They'd torture me if I let them.

I do believe in energy. Einstein said energy cannot be created or destroyed. When we die, that energy goes somewhere. I'd like to think Jeff Ebner's energy travels well.

We can't see all things, but we can feel them. When my dad died, I drove my aging Ford Taurus—a car I got from our junkyard—from Columbus to Springfield to pick up my dad's 1988 Mercedes S class. I loved that car. Leather seats, as luxurious as an ancient vehicle could be. The Date Car, my dad called it.

As I drove the Mercedes from Springfield to my mom's house, I caught an odor pouring from the passenger seat. It was as distinct and obvious as Jeff Ebner's personality. Having spent lots of hours in that very seat, to and from my mom's house and rugby practice, I knew exactly what the stink was.

Gas, passed. A parting gift from my dad. Some of Einstein's energy, appearing in a form only my dad would dream of conjuring up. *That's a strong finish, Eb.*

I chuckled. Somewhere, I'm sure, he was roaring.

Acknowledgments

I want to personally thank Urban Meyer for writing the foreword. Your words exemplify a clear understanding of who I am and where I come from. But more important, I want to thank you for encouraging me to tell my story as seriously as you did.

I want to thank my friends and my family for never trying to hold me back, and for their support through all of my endeavors across the country and around the world—I always had a familiar face to look for, no matter where I was or what I was doing.

I want to thank all of my teammates and coaches through all the years, through all the sports I've played. I took something from all of you—whether it was specific details in the sport, how to be a professional, inspiring words, determination in your duties, or your silent, consistent work ethic, all of you taught me lessons.

I want to thank and acknowledge my stepmother, Amy, for her patience with my dad's and my relationship. I know it wasn't always easy when I was around, or when my dad would leave you to come see me as frequently as he did. It took a lot of strength and patience, and I appreciate you for that.

I want to thank my wife, Chelsey, for all of her support throughout my entire career. For putting her life and career on hold for the sake of our relationship. The sacrifices you made early in our relationship and continue to make confirm the type of love we share. You've been a great example of selflessness and a major part of my support system, someone who I could lean on through it all.

Last, I want to thank my mother, Nancy. You raised me to be a good person, and you have supported me through everything in my life. You showed me strength when I needed it the most. I would not be where I am today or have done any of the things I have done without you.